"As a Christian who also knows same-sex desire firsthand, I would put a few things differently from how Ed Shaw does here. But that doesn't stop me from applauding this biblically thorough, evangelistically zealous, humbly self-disclosing and pastorally compassionate defense of traditional Christian sexual ethics. Ed Shaw's life and teaching are an inspiring variation on what the church throughout history has celebrated as consecrated, holy virginity. May his tribe increase!"

Wesley Hill, assistant professor of biblical studies, Trinity School for Ministry, Ambridge, Pennsylvania, author of *Washed and Waiting*

"Ed Shaw shares his story and perspective in this book with deep sincerity, conviction and honesty. He makes a profound contribution to the conversation about same-sex attraction. I am so glad I read this book and I wholeheartedly recommend it."

Amy Orr-Ewing, Director of Programmes, Oxford Centre for Christian Apologetics (OCCA), UK Director, RZIM Zacharias Trust

"Read this book to learn about the faith and life of a devout celibate man. Readers will surely vary in their response to Shaw's theological views, but all will deepen their understanding and respect for celibacy as a spiritual practice and will come away challenged to build stronger supports for all people, married and single, in their local churches."

Jenell Paris, professor of anthropology, Messiah College, author of *The End of Sexual Identity*

"The big idea of Ed Shaw's book is simple: the church must make the biblical commands on sexuality seem plausible again. He calls all of us to repentance and wisely shows us a better way to battle sin, to understand sufferers and to proclaim truth with grace. Even those who don't agree with every jot and tittle will find something to be challenged and encouraged by on nearly every page. I highly recommend this clear, courageous and compassionate book."

Justin Taylor, coauthor, *The Final Days of Jesus*, blogger, "Between Two Worlds"

"*Same-Sex Attraction and the Church* is a must-read for all Christians. Pastor Shaw lives out what it means to apply faith to the facts of unwanted, unchosen and sometimes unshakable same-sex attraction. This powerful book meets readers at the heart level, manifesting a positive understanding of the sacrifices of the Christian life. And because it is so disarmingly positive about the Christian art of dying to self, it sings a clarion call, shedding new light on this sacred truth: the real gospel imparts a will-influencing, heart-changing light into the souls of men and women and the community that we create together. . . . I love this book."

Rosaria Butterfield, author of *The Secret Thoughts of An Unlikely Convert*

"Our culture places sex at the heart of identity and fulfillment. But Ed Shaw has discovered in the God of the gospel a pleasure that is greater and an identity that is richer than anything we can create for ourselves. Over against the false choice of embracing homosexuality or ignoring it, he gives us the category of 'same-sex-attracted-but-in-Christ.' In doing so, he shows the power of the gospel to direct us all away from both indulging our sins and denying the reality of our temptations. The fidelity to truth and loving wisdom in this book is exactly what we all need right now."

Michael Horton, professor of theology, Westminster Seminary California

"Ed Shaw identifies the primary obstacle to a Christian sexual ethic in today's culture. It is not that the culture weighs Christian arguments and finds them wanting, but rather that the culture cannot imagine any alternative to sexual autonomy. In this book, Shaw pastorally and wisely shows how to apply a Christian vision of marriage and sexuality to those with attraction to the same sex. The book is a welcome vehicle for discipleship for the whole church to help us to bear one another's burdens."

Russell D. Moore, Southern Baptist Ethics & Religious Liberty Commission

SAME-SEX ATTRACTION

and the CHURCH

*The Surprising Plausibility
of the Celibate Life*

ED SHAW

IVP Books

An imprint of InterVarsity Press
Downers Grove, Illinois

InterVarsity Press
P.O. Box 1400, Downers Grove, IL 60515-1426
ivpress.com
email@ivpress.com

InterVarsity Press® is the book-publishing division of InterVarsity Christian Fellowship/USA®, a movement of students and faculty active on campus at hundreds of universities, colleges and schools of nursing in the United States of America, and a member movement of the International Fellowship of Evangelical Students. For information about local and regional activities, visit intervarsity.org.

All Scripture quotations, unless otherwise indicated, are taken from THE HOLY BIBLE, NEW INTERNATIONAL VERSION®, NIV® Copyright © 1973, 1978, 1984, 2011 by Biblica, Inc.™ Used by permission. All rights reserved worldwide.

While any stories in this book are true, some names and identifying information may have been changed to protect the privacy of individuals.

Cover design: Cindy Kiple
Interior design: Beth McGill

Images: © Chalabala/iStockphoto

ISBN 978-0-8308-4451-7 (print)
ISBN 978-0-8308-9979-1 (digital)

Printed in the United States of America ∞

 As a member of the Green Press Initiative, InterVarsity Press is committed to protecting the environment and to the responsible use of natural resources. To learn more, visit greenpressinitiative.org.

Library of Congress Cataloging-in-Publication Data

Shaw, Ed (Pastor), author.
  Same-sex attraction and the church : the surprising plausibility of the celibate life / Ed Shaw.
    pages cm
  Includes bibliographical references.
  ISBN 978-0-8308-4451-7 (pbk. : alk. paper)
  1. Homosexuality—Religious aspects—Christianity. 2. Homosexuality—Biblical teaching.
3. Celibacy—Christianity. I. Title.
  BR115.H6S53 2015
  241'.664—dc23

                                                                            2015033914

P   20   19   18   17   16   15   14   13   12   11   10   9   8   7   6   5   4   3   2

Y   32   31   30   29   28   27   26   25   24   23   22   21   20   19   18   17   16

To Mum and Dad

With thanks for showing me

the plausibility of life following Jesus

Contents

FOREWORD

Vaughan Roberts

This is an important book, one of the most important I have read in recent years. I tend to discount such comments as the kind of hyperbole that is expected in a foreword written by an author's friend, so let me stress, I really do mean it.

This is not, as you may imagine, simply a conservative book, addressed only to believers who experience same-sex attraction, urging us to hold the biblical line on that one subject. It is, above all, radical, challenging all believers to a comprehensive reformation of thinking and behavior. Let me tell you why I like it so much.

First, it is a sensitive book. It is pastorally sensitive, as one might expect from a writer who is open about his own experience of same-sex attraction. His honesty about what that actually feels like is refreshing. He gets it. That matters for those of us in the same situation. But, equally important, Ed Shaw is culturally sensitive. He recognizes that the gods of our age—even for many Christians who claim to believe that the Bible is the ultimate authority—have a greater influence on their ethical stance than biblical interpretation, whether consciously acknowledged or not. It is not so much that minds have been con-

vinced by new interpretations but that hearts have been cap-
tured by the assumptions of individualism.

In a world and, far too often, a church in which self-expression
and self-fulfillment are largely unquestioned values, the or-
thodox Christian position on homosexuality can feel both un-
sustainable and even immoral. In this context, few will be convinced of the rightness of that teaching, however well the biblical
case is argued, unless they are persuaded of its plausibility.

Ed Shaw understands that this demands a book that does not
simply focus the mind on the interpretation of a few key texts
but also addresses the heart and its underlying and often unrec-
ognized convictions.

The second striking feature of this book is that it is so positive.
As Ed argues, the "Just Say No!" approach to homosexuality is
no longer compelling—if it ever was. What he offers us instead
is a positive vision of the possibility of a vibrant and fulfilling life
in fellowship with Christ for same-sex attracted Christians, even
if it does mean missing out on sex and marriage.

Of course, there will be suffering at times, but how could we
expect otherwise in following the one who entered his glory via
crucifixion and called on his disciples to travel the same road by
denying themselves and taking up the cross? But what we are
asked to give up is nothing compared with what we are invited to
receive, both now and in the future. Life with Christ does involve
sacrifice, as in all relationships, but it is defined ultimately not by
what is denied but by what or, better, *who* is embraced. The saying
no is preceded and enveloped by the yes we say to Christ, which
is a response to his loving YES to us. He came to bring us life, not
a form of living death, and he died to make that possible.

We may experience the equivalent of what Ed calls his "kitchen
floor moments," when everything seems bleak, but in Christ and

the wonder of all that God gives us in him, we have ample reason to get up off the floor, persevere and rejoice. He calls us not to teeth-gritting stoicism but to faith-filled joy in sorrow and hope in affliction.

The final reason I like this book so much is that it is punchy. The tone is never aggressive or hectoring, but you can sense the author's passion and righteous frustration. His sights are not set on the predictable target—compromising liberals—but on those who belong to his own evangelical tribe.

Rather than simply accusing others of being unbiblical, we need to examine our own tradition against the standard of God's Word. While claiming to resist the idols of hedonism and relativism, have we not too often entered into an unholy alliance with self, the modern idol that is worshipped most fervently of all? The result, too often, is a perversion of authentic Christianity that has little room for costly sacrifice and leaves the individual on the throne, rather than the living God.

And in resisting the sexual revolution, have we not so exalted marriage and the nuclear family that we have marginalized or ignored the Bible's vision of the church as God's family and singleness, whether chosen or not, as a positive vocation? The current controversy over homosexuality in the church gives us an opportunity to recognize and repent of these and other "missteps," which have added immeasurably to the sense of the implausibility of the life to which we are calling some of our number.

From the world's perspective, Christ's call to a wholehearted, sacrificial discipleship seems implausibly unattractive for anyone, regardless of their sexuality or particular circumstances. If we are to persevere in the life of discipleship ourselves and persuade anyone else to join us, we must somehow communicate that what is offered is not a set of rules but a dynamic relationship with the living God.

We could never live such a life in isolation, but as Christians, we have not been left on our own. We know God as our Father, who is lovingly sovereign over all things and is at work in and through even the hardest moments and aspects of our lives for our good and his glory. We know Christ as our Lord and Savior, the one who asks us to take up his cross and follow him, having already laid down his life for us and offered us infinitely more than he ever demands. And we know the Spirit as Comforter, who is with us every step of the way and calls us into a life of deep and satisfying intimacy in union with Christ and in the fellowship of the church.

When lived with this God at the center, the Christian life is not only plausible; it is wonderful.

The Plausibility Problem

Peter

Meet seventeen-year-old Peter. He's a good Christian and an enthusiastic member of a church youth group. The eldest son of a deacon and the kids' church coordinator, he plays electric guitar in the worship band, runs the Bible club at his school, is doing well academically and is well known locally as an increasingly promising competitive swimmer. He's the sort of high-achieving Christian young man that convinces people that the church might just have a future.

But since the beginning of puberty, Peter has been consistently attracted to other guys. What he hoped was just a phase hasn't passed—despite his prayers and best efforts to feel something for girls. He's become an expert at faking heterosexuality, but struggles at youth group to push away the attention of some of the girls while trying not to focus too much attention on one of the guys.

The church youth group prides itself on its good Bible teaching. Its leaders take their responsibilities seriously, especially when it comes to explaining the church's traditional teaching on sex and relationships. Peter has been told repeatedly that sex is for the marriage of a man and a woman. Until then, he's to resist the temptation to be sexually active in both thought and deed. So, for instance, he's been told what to do when he's sexually attracted to a woman—of how it's not wrong to notice beauty but of the dangers of a second look and the mental undressing that can follow. But the problem is, he's attracted to men, so even the first look, the first attraction, feels wrong to him—he's been paralyzed with guilt by the feelings brought on by watching that guy he likes undress in the dorm on a church weekend away. Because the one thing that he's heard about homosexuality is that it is all wrong—a no-go area for a good Christian like him.

But boy, does Peter want to have sex. He's growing up in one of the most sexualized cultures since pre-Christendom. It's what teenage life is all about, according to the magazines he reads, the TV shows he watches and the conversations that happen in the locker room. It's what shows you've grown up. It's what makes you a real man. Even in his youth group, it's talked up to be the most amazing, life-changing experience. A young couple on the youth leadership team were recently interviewed up front and shared how grateful they were that they'd waited to have sex until they were married. Talking to the youth group guys in a males-only session afterward, the husband said sex was the best experience he'd ever had—God was so good to have created something so pleasurable. It would be that good for them too—if they kept it for marriage.

But Peter won't be getting any if he sticks with what he's been told, if he lives in the light of the Bible's teaching. And that seems unreasonable (to say the least) for seventeen-year-old Peter. Sex is everywhere. His desire for it is overwhelming. And his church says no to that—forever.

At the same time, those magazines, those TV shows, if not yet the locker-room conversations, are telling him to go with his feelings. His favorite TV show has a gay character that he both finds attractive and would love to be like—totally unashamed of his sexuality and getting loads of sex. A couple of furtive Google searches have shown him that there are Christians who think that permanent, stable and faithful gay relationships are right in God's sight. He might be able to get the sex he wants after all. And remain a Christian. He wants both.

Jane

Now meet Jane. She's in her late thirties. She's had a series of disastrous relationships with men—including a brief marriage that ended after his adultery. She became a Christian soon afterward and has thrown herself into church life: she serves the coffee on Sunday mornings, she's part of the welcome team and she coordinates the church's soup kitchen for the homeless. At last year's Christmas Eve service, she was up at the front giving her testimony as someone whose life has been totally transformed by Jesus. She's one of her church's few recent success stories.

But alongside her church family, a close friendship with a non-Christian woman at work has been one of her chief supports in recent years and, much to Jane's surprise, their close relationship has recently become sexual. Everyone has noticed how much happier she's been—her small group is praising God that he's answered their prayers for her, not knowing the cause.

Jane's church has taken a firm stand in opposing gay "marriage." Jane hadn't realized that same-sex sexual relationships were wrong before. So she was soon at the pastor's house asking for advice on behalf of "a Christian friend" of hers who had recently become sexually involved with a same-sex colleague. The pastor was clear on the need to call for repentance and to separate from the Christian friend if she didn't change her behavior soon.

Jane is devastated. What she wants most in life is to settle down with someone she loves and who loves her back. As she left the pastor's home, she saw his wife and small children baking cookies together in the kitchen, and she longed to have that sort of settled home life. She's always wanted kids and she's really loved being involved in the lives of her girlfriend's children from a previous relationship. What she had so often dreamed of had finally come true.

But if she does as she's been told, she will be ending things with her girlfriend tomorrow. Ending the best human relationship she's ever been in. And that seems so unreasonable. So unreasonable for her pastor to deny her what *he's* got. For him to say that something that feels so right is so wrong.

She knows what her girlfriend will say. She's been very respectful of Jane's religious side but will tell her to ignore what the pastor said. And her appeal will be powerfully backed up with all that she offers. A shared home, a family life, an end to loneliness, the physical affection that Jane needs so much. With her girlfriend gone, Jane will be back to her one-bedroom apartment, irregular and painful visits to church families for Sunday lunch, the single life, and looking forward to the greeting at church because it's the only physical touch she ever gets there.

Our Response

It's the Peters and Janes in our churches who are causing many evangelicals to lose their confidence in the Bible's teaching on sex and marriage. It's the real people like them who are tempting an increasing number of evangelicals to "go liberal" on homosexuality. You might be one of them. How can you look Peter in the eye and deny him sex forever? How can we ask Jane to turn her back on the one human relationship that has brought her joy? It just won't seem plausible to them. It doesn't sound that reasonable to us either.

And what doesn't help them or us much is the standard evangelical response to what they're facing. We've basically adopted the slogan from the 1980s anti-drugs song "Just Say No!" That's often all we have to say—exacerbated by the proof-text parade if anyone raises any objections:

Do not have sexual relations with a man as one does with a woman; that is detestable. (Leviticus 18:22)

If a man has sexual relations with a man as one does with a woman, both of them have done what is detestable. They are to be put to death; their blood will be on their own heads. (Leviticus 20:13)

Because of this, God gave them over to shameful lusts. Even their women exchanged natural sexual relations for unnatural ones. In the same way the men also abandoned natural relations with women and were inflamed with lust for one another. Men committed shameful acts with other men, and received in themselves the due penalty for their error. (Romans 1:26-27)

Or do you not know that wrongdoers will not inherit the kingdom of God? Do not be deceived: Neither the sexually immoral nor idolaters nor adulterers nor men who have sex with men nor thieves nor the greedy nor drunkards nor slanderers nor swindlers will inherit the kingdom of God. (1 Corinthians 6:9-10)

> We also know that the law is made not for the righteous
> but for lawbreakers and rebels, the ungodly and sinful,
> the unholy and irreligious, for those who kill their fathers
> or mothers, for murderers, for the sexually immoral, for
> those practicing homosexuality, for slave traders and liars
> and perjurers—and for whatever else is contrary to the
> sound doctrine that conforms to the gospel concerning
> the glory of the blessed God, which he entrusted to me.
> (1 Timothy 1:9-11)

That used to convince. That used to be a plausible argument for most. To be an evangelical has always meant holding to the truth of "the divine inspiration of Holy Scripture as originally given and its supreme authority in all matters of faith and conduct."[1] And when it comes to homosexual practice, those Scriptures are pretty clear. Evangelicals like clarity, and those verses were more than enough clarity for many, for years. We all knew where we stood.

But that is no longer the case. Things have changed. Although older generations of evangelical Christians might remain wedded to the church's traditional teaching, younger generations are deserting it in droves. I've spoken to countless pastors in their forties and fifties who remain committed to what the church has always taught—but nearly all of them have said their children don't even get where they're coming from on this issue. You might be one of that younger generation yourself. A generation changing their minds on homosexuality today, not because they've suddenly revised their opinion of the cultural context of Leviticus, the meaning of "unnatural" in Romans 1, the nature of homosexual practice in Corinth or the translation of the Greek words in 1 Timothy, but because what those texts demand just doesn't seem plausible anymore. It's people, not theology, that seem to be powering the rejection of the traditional Christian ethic. It's Peter and Jane—and others like them—not the Hebrew and Greek.

Many of us might not like this changing reality, but it is the reality we face. Ask around and you'll keep encountering it. I keep hearing of same-sex attracted Christians who think that what the Bible asks is just not doable in today's world. And who then, only when they've concluded this, find the books, the sermons, the theologians, that will allow them to dismiss what the Bible teaches. Their friends, family and churches then tend to walk the same well-trodden path soon after—simply out of their love and concern for them. It's in the whole area of practical plausibility rather than biblical exegesis where things have really changed in recent years. That's why the landscape is changing so rapidly—whether we like it or not.

Peter and Jane's Response

And so this is my best bet on what will happen to Peter and Jane (unless we seek to help them more). Peter will head to college and enter a world in which it is easy to embrace his same-sex attraction. A friendship with a guy will grow into something else, and his Christian friends won't know what to say. The student leader at the "solid" church that his youth leader sent him to might say something, but it will be easy for Peter to switch churches and find one that will turn a blind eye, or one that will be totally affirming. And his contemporaries from the youth group will struggle to see what the problem is, will meet his boyfriend, see how happy Peter is and change their minds too—a response that will soon ripple out through his home church.

Jane will soon stop going to her church. She has been asked to give up too much. She will move in with her girlfriend and her name will be quickly wiped from church directory. Talk of her at her small group will produce embarrassed silence, but outside its meetings, a number will conclude that it's great she's so happy now and will be baffled by how the church has treated her. Bumping into her and her girlfriend and their children at the local park will convince many that what they now have together is something the church should have not condemned but encouraged, even blessed. Just look at how much they love each other!

That's the most plausible outcome, isn't it? That's what will almost certainly happen to them. And we struggle to blame them. What sounds totally implausible today is asking them to turn their backs on those same-sex sexual relationships and to embrace lifelong singleness. The evangelical church's basic message to them—"Just Say No!"—just doesn't have any real credibility anymore. It embarrasses many of us to even ask them to do it. It sounds positively unhealthy. It lacks any traction in today's world— simply producing incredulity from the majority. Melinda Selmys (a Catholic who experiences same-sex attraction) communicates this well:

> Negative chastity, the kind of chastity that limits itself to saying "Thou shalt not," has consistently failed to persuade the postmodern world because it is *madness*. The vast majority of people will eat things that are designated "unclean" by their religion or "unhealthy" by their doctors when faced with starvation. In most cases it's not even voluntary. Unless you have strengthened your will to a superhuman extent it's not possible to starve yourself to death. Likewise, unless you've devoted a huge number of character points to picking up the "Stoic" superpower you will simply not be able to endure the kind of social starvation that negative chastity demands in the contemporary world.[2]

We have to start responding with more than "Just Say No!" It doesn't have enough power in our modern world. The single life we are calling Peter and Jane to today was plausible in the past— but it seems so unreasonable today. It just won't be enough to persuade Peter and Jane and those who, rightly, feel for them. Unless, that is, we solve what I'm calling . . .

A Plausibility Problem

We have a plausibility issue: what the Bible clearly teaches sounds unreasonable to many of us today. And so it is (not unreasonably!) being rejected all over the place. A few high-profile leaders in our churches have already broken ranks. The worrying silence of a number of other key leaders and churches should prepare us for more and more sudden departures from the biblical teaching that sex is for marriage and that marriage is the lifelong union of a man and a woman. You might, of course, be near changing your mind yourself.

What can we do about it? Well, this is where this book is designed to help. Its basic premise is simple: we just have to make what the Bible clearly commands seem plausible again. We need to remind ourselves, and remind Peter and Jane, that Jesus says this to us all: "I have come that they may have life, and have it to the full" (John 10:10). And Jesus always speaks the truth. If that doesn't sound possible, plausible for people like Peter and Jane today, it's not because Jesus has gotten anything wrong but because we have.

The Solution

This is where it all begins to be positive! For, it turns out, the reason that the Bible's teaching on homosexuality sounds so unreasonable is because of a whole number of missteps that the church itself has taken over the years; a whole host of ways in which evangelicals have become too shaped by the world around us. Correct our mistakes, and what Jesus says about sex and relationships will become more plausible, will sound, again, more like life to the full. And that will be good news for all of us.

And that is what the rest of this book seeks to do: highlight these missteps so that we can begin to rid ourselves of this plausibility problem. We can do this in ways that will not only benefit the likes of Peter and Jane but will also benefit the whole church too; for these missteps haven't just damaged the same-sex attracted members of our churches, they've crippled us all. We will all be called to repentance for ways in which we have, unintentionally, made Jesus' way sound like a bad deal rather than the best way for any human life to be lived—which it is!

2

The Plausibility Problem and Me

A Personal Statement

Before we turn to the missteps, I need to make a personal statement. I write this book as an evangelical Christian who experiences same-sex attraction. Ever since the beginning of puberty, my sexual desires have been focused on some members of my own sex. What I thought might be just a teenage phase (I'd read *Brideshead Revisited*)[1] has never gone away and I remain exclusively same-sex attracted in my mid/late thirties, despite all my best efforts and prayers to change.

So the plausibility problem is my problem. It's not just one that "friends of mine" are facing out there (although I have many friends who are)—it's an issue that I live with every day of my life. And so let me tell you that it is quite a problem for an evangelical Christian to have. I believe that the Bible is God's inspired (and thus inerrant and authoritative) Word to the people he's both created and redeemed. Through its pages, my loving Father God tells me everything I need to know about everything that matters to him (2 Timothy 3:16-17). And those pages very clearly say that homosexual practice is wrong in his sight—remember the proof-text parade in the previous chapter. I am absolutely convinced of this, despite my own same-sex attraction and those who now tell me God never really said that or has recently changed his mind. But it's not even those famous individual verses that I find most persuasive. I'm with my friend Wes Hill (another same-sex attracted Christian) when he writes this:

> In the end, what keeps me on the path I've chosen is not so much individual proof texts from Scripture or the sheer weight of the church's traditional teaching against homosexual practice. Instead, it is, I think, those texts and traditions and teachings *as I see them from within the true story of what God has done in Jesus Christ*—and the whole perspective on life and the world that flows from that story, as expressed definitively in Scripture. Like a piece from a jigsaw puzzle finally locked into its rightful place, the Bible and the church's no to homosexual behavior make sense— it has the ring of truth, as J. B. Phillips once said of the New Testament—when I look at it as one piece within the larger Christian narrative. I abstain from homosexual behavior because of the power of the Scriptural story.[2]

Do you want to see those texts and teachings from that fuller perspective? You could read my brief appendix 1 at the back of this book on the subject now or, better, when you've finished this book, read some of the fuller treatments of the subject listed in the Recommended Reading section. The more I've dug into the unfolding story of the whole Bible and explored the full sweep of church history, the more I've found that my conviction that sex is just for the marriage of a man and a woman has grown. Reading some of the recently published revisionist writings has only served to strengthen this conviction—each time I've put myself in a spiritual brace position, expecting some new biblical interpretation to floor me, but the opposite has always been true (read appendix 2 to find out why I've found them so unconvincing).

And yet, running in parallel with these increasingly strong convictions, every day of my adult life I have found myself instinctively sexually attracted to a certain type of beautiful man. The fact that I have never slept with any of them doesn't help me when Jesus condemns sexual fantasy in his Sermon on the Mount (Matthew 5:27-28). I might not have actually had sex with a man, but I've imagined myself having sex with many over the years. There seems to be a massive gap between what I believe intellectually and what I instinctively feel and think day by day.

A Changing Context

That was complicated enough to cope with back in the 1990s, when I was first coming to terms with my sexuality. The issues of guilt and lack of assurance that my sexuality has often brought plagued me for years—and almost derailed me spiritually at times. I sometimes wondered whether striving to live in the light of the Bible's teaching was plausible as I struggled in silence. I told no one of my same-sex attraction until my late twenties.

But what helped me was that, back then, embracing a homosexual lifestyle was clearly a no-go area for an evangelical Christian like me. Although a member of staff at my evangelical college did publish a book articulating a new, more liberal approach, he was almost a lone voice at the time. No one in the campus ministry or at my Anglican church in Durham would have publicly backed his approach to Scripture. My Christian friends were united in their rejection of what he wrote. The parameters set out for me were crystal clear—celibacy and a daily battle to avoid even a hint of sexual immorality in what I thought or did (Ephesians 5:3). The "Just Say No!" message had not yet reached its best-before date—it still had some power. And although I found the consequences of that clarity immensely hard, the lack of ambiguity was incredibly helpful. It made the choice I'd taken seem plausible.

As we've already noted, things are very different today. That is most obvious in the world outside the Christian church, where the gay community has moved from being a disregarded minority to an increasingly influential part of mainstream public life in just under twenty years. But that's also true within the evangelical church—if at a slightly different pace. We are, as ethicist Russell Moore has put it, "the slow train sexual revolutionaries."[3] Even within our circles, that lone figure from my college has been followed by an increasing number of revisionist voices coming from within the evangelical fold. There are now evangelical leaders like Rob Bell and David Gushee who would talk positively of permanent, faithful and stable same-sex sexual relationships. Some would say that I could marry the man of my dreams in their churches. And then even become a bishop! I can now, according to some, have it all. Their message has been completely reversed: "Just Say Yes!"

This has been reflected in the changing attitudes of some of my Christian friends and family too. Once signed up to the same theological perspective as me, some have now told me that I don't need to stick to what the Bible teaches any more. When I've said I still want to, they have replied that they will be there when I eventually get with the program and realize how we've misinterpreted those verses and misapplied them to homosexuality today.

And how tempting that is! I would dearly love to stay within evangelicalism and do that with a beautiful man by my side. It is such an attractive prospect. No more self-denial—instead I can be self-indulgent *and* have that blessed by Jesus! It would be a win-win situation. How plausible it is to imagine life to the full in that situation; how difficult it is to imagine a similar life to the full all by myself. The world outside the church would definitely affirm me—but now many of my brothers and sisters in Christ would too.

So the environment in which I'm trying to be faithful to the church's traditional teaching is much harsher now than it ever was before. And that makes my life even harder than it was before. Think for a moment of your greatest besetting sin. The thing God asks you not to think or do, but you keep on thinking or doing. Consider how much your efforts to say no to it would be undermined if suddenly you were told it wasn't wrong any more or, at the very least, if a few voices started to raise doubts in your mind. When next tempted, things would be much more challenging, wouldn't they? Why resist thinking or doing that if it isn't really a sin anymore? If Jesus didn't mind—if Jesus would actually approve!

Welcome to one of the fiercest challenges of my life. Go back just a decade and I had almost unanimous support from within the evangelical community for the life I'm living. I knew that even a permanent, stable and faithful sexual relationship with another man would have serious consequences for my place in the church. So it was much easier not even to consider it as an option. Now the possibility keeps coming to mind. It often seems much more plausible and so much more attractive.

A Different World

Now reflect on how much harder it must be if you are a same-sex attracted Christian a couple of decades or so younger than me. It helps that I'm used to the clear parameters of the evangelicalism of the past; I have built my life around them and received (mostly) loving encouragement to do that and gentle warnings not to reject it. But if I were growing up today, I fear I'd have very little help of that sort.

Many evangelical churches and organizations (perhaps including those that you are part of) are keeping totally silent on the issue, for fear of being labeled homophobic and hindering their evangelism. With such silence from those supposed to be providing them with biblical pastoral care, it is inevitable that younger same-sex attracted evangelicals, repelled by the insensitive stridency of some more conservative groups, will go with the liberal flow of contemporary society and embrace the attractively permissive line of some other Christians. This seems unstoppable. It is hard to believe that without the anchor of clearer Bible teaching they will resist the ebbing tide running in the opposite direction.

And that's one reason why I'm writing this book. To remind myself that it is still plausible to stick to what the Bible teaches and hopefully to persuade some other same-sex attracted evangelicals too. People like Peter and Jane. Perhaps someone like you. We need to rebuild a plausibility structure so that we can live in the light of the Bible's clear teaching.

But we can't do that on our own. That's because the life to which same-sex attracted Christians are called will only seem possible if we all help in the rebuilding of that plausibility structure by recognizing and recalibrating our churches in the light of the missteps that the rest of this book will describe. Without a joint effort, we won't ever succeed. That's the other main reason why I'm writing this book: to enlist the wider church's active support for our same-sex attracted sisters and brothers. So what follows is relevant for all of us.

You see, when a same-sex attracted Christian embraces a gay identity and lifestyle, we need to recognize that it might be, to some extent, not just their fault but ours too. Our response should not just be to shake our heads sadly and call on them to repent but to look inside at how our attitudes and actions might have pushed them over the edge. I'm not absolving them of responsibility, but I am challenging the rest of the church to accept theirs. To ask ourselves the question: Are there things that we might need to actively repent of too? Remember Martin Luther's repentance-promoting words: "There is no greater sinner than the Christian church." I think that's a fact particularly well illustrated in this area, and I'll be setting out the ways in which we all desperately need to change in the rest of this book. Expect to find that you will need to correct your own beliefs and behavior in the light of what follows—and please keep assessing how your own church helps or hinders the same-sex attracted Christians in your midst. I will end every chapter with a question to help you do this.

Another Personal Statement

This plausibility problem is pretty obviously a deeply personal and emotional issue for me! I need to apologize in advance if that means it often sounds as if I have an axe to grind and that I'm grinding it on you. I do feel quite strongly on this issue, and you'll need to watch that I don't go too far. It's also why I'll be regularly incorporating the perspectives of others—I don't want what follows to sound like a purely personal rant, so I've included their words too.

But I hope that by now, if you didn't already, you are beginning to feel that this is a deeply personal and emotional issue for you too. That what you perhaps thought was just a problem for a very small minority within the evangelical church is actually one that we all need to do something about—not just for the sake of the few but to benefit us all. If you've ever secretly hoped that both the issue of same-sex attraction and same-sex attracted people would just go away, I hope you've realized by now that it and they won't. So we urgently need to think about it more constructively and help them more compassionately, remembering that it's so often been similarly controversial issues and people that God has used to conform his imperfect church more and more to the image of his perfect Son.

MISSTEP #1

"Your identity is your sexuality."

A Christian friend of mine who recently shared his experience of same-sex attraction with his church family was confronted by this question from a younger person: "Aren't you just saying you're gay?" And at one level, he was. That would have been an easier way to communicate it—using language that we are all familiar with today. Talk of experiencing same-sex attraction is a little harder for people today to grasp—what exactly did he mean? He'd confused some people.

My friend was choosing his language carefully. And I choose to do the same—both in my everyday life and in writing this book. Saying, "I'm gay" is—at one level—the quickest way of clarifying my sexual orientation in our world today. People instantly think they know what I mean. But the problem is that they don't. They will equate me saying, "I'm gay" with me embracing a gay lifestyle and identity, which I'm not. They'll expect me soon to be introducing them to my partner Brian or to be thrilled if they match me up with their gay friend Barry, which I won't be. The statement needs so much clarification so soon that it's actually easier to use different language (and it's not just Christians like me who are doing this).[1]

Of course, some people quickly sniff out shame in all these (to them) pedantic semantics—but I just want to communicate effectively. If I say, "I'm gay," people think they know what I mean and don't ask me any more questions. But if I say, "I experience same-sex attraction," they're confused and so ask me more. It allows me to communicate accurately what I want to say about my sexuality. I tend to think it's one of those areas of life where accuracy is quite important.

It certainly helps you battle the stereotypes that rain down on you once you say you are attracted to people of the same sex. Anything that gets people asking you questions rather than thinking that they now know exactly which box to put you in allows you to explain your own unique sexuality and personality properly. I've been amazed by the people who have treated me as a stereotype rather than an individual since I've been more open about my sexuality, so any language that gets people thinking outside the box is, I think, a good thing. It also helps limit the invitations to bad musicals (to name and shame just one of the stereotypes).

Labels Matter

But it's not *The Phantom of the Opera* that I'm trying to avoid most. What I most want to avoid is any other identity that might attempt to displace my fundamental identity as a Christian. Because the thing that defines me most in life is not my sexuality but my status—in Christ—as a son of God.

Isn't that totally undeserved new status the most wonderful thing about becoming a Christian? Being adopted into God's own family through trust in his Son, Jesus! Unsurprisingly, John opens his Gospel with this offer:

> Yet to all who did receive him, to those who believed in his name, he gave the right to become children of God— children born not of natural descent, nor of human decision or a husband's will, but born of God. (John 1:12-13)

This Gospel tells me that I am—in Jesus—a child of God. That is why I can call him Father. That is why I can call Jesus my brother. That is what his Spirit confirms by dwelling inside of me. That is who I am: God's own dear son.

And thinking like that is crucial to living the Christian life. Why? Listen to pastor Kevin DeYoung:

> If I had to summarize New Testament ethics in one sentence, here's how I would put it: *be who you are.* That may sound strange, almost heretical, given our culture's emphasis on being true to yourself. But like so many of the worst errors in the world, this one represents a truth powerfully perverted. When people say, "Relax, you were born that way." or "Quit trying to be something you're not and just be the real you," they are stumbling upon something very biblical. God *does* want you to be the real you. He *does* want you to be true to yourself. But the "you" he's talking about is the "you" that you are by grace, not by nature. You may want to read through that last sentence again because the difference between living in sin and living in righteousness depends on getting that sentence right. God doesn't say, "Relax, you were born this way." But he does say, "Good news, you were reborn another way." [2]

Who is the true Ed Shaw? Not Ed Shaw as the society around me defines me. Not even Ed Shaw as I see myself. But the Ed Shaw who is both seen and defined by God as his son! That is the identity I want people around me to hear of. And that is how I increasingly need to see myself. Why?

Well, it beats all the other possible ways of defining me because it's a divinely constructed identity, not a human one. People only started being labeled as homosexuals back in the nineteenth century (philosopher Michel Foucault traced its first use to an article published in 1870[3]). Using the term "gay" to define yourself is even more recent—a generation or two back, it was just a woman's name or a happy feeling you might have for an afternoon. Like all human language, these terms have changed their meanings and will, no doubt, evolve some more. But what will never change is my status as a child of God. Ephesians 1 tells me I've been that in God's sight since before the creation of the world. "Child of God" is a permanent label that he has personally chosen for me and, as a result, it is the most accurate way of defining me. It should have no rivals.

If this label did reign supreme in my heart, it would certainly help me. Let me show you how. Yesterday I sought out a trailer for a film in which an attractive man was half-naked at times. As I was repenting to my Father God afterwards, what was the devil telling me? "This is who you are! The sort of man who spends time lusting after brief glimpses of this man's torso. Call yourself a Christian? You can't be and enjoy doing this!" Where does the evil one always take the battle? Straight to my identity! That's where the battle is fiercest, and that's why I need to hold on to my identity in Christ so much. Yesterday I had to keep saying to myself: "This isn't the real you! You are God's son. God has permanently made you that through the death of Jesus. You shouldn't have done what you just did, but it changes nothing about you!" Every day of my life, I need to keep on saying that. And, of course, you do too.

All of this also matters so much because we tend to live out the identities that people give us or that we give ourselves. They can gain a powerful hold on our lives. People who are repeatedly told or think "You're stupid" or "You're ugly" start to behave as if they were—sometimes even when there is plenty of evidence to the contrary. Words have the power to shape us and make (or unmake) us. So what I want to hear and think most of all is: "I'm God's son"—not: "I'm gay."

I'm not saying that people become same-sex attracted because they are told they're gay—or will stop if they're not. But I *am* saying that I don't think it's helpful for Christians to take it up as a label. I have evangelical friends who have but who are most definitely not embracing the full identity and lifestyle. But I do worry about the negative pastoral implications of that decision (as they probably worry about the negative evangelistic implications of mine).[4]

I think it can restrict our openness to the potential of change. I have friends who would testify to this—that labeling themselves as gay put them in a manmade box that then limited their expectations of what God could do in their lives and lessened their expectation of change. I reckon anything that undermines my hope in the power of the gospel is something I want to steer clear of as much as I possibly can.

So I think that a Christian should be wary of doing anything that might root his or her identity in their sexuality. We need to be countercultural on this: our identity is, instead, to be firmly rooted in Christ.

Sinners or Saints?

But where's the theological misstep that the evangelical church has made here? Have you missed it? Here it is: it's the danger that some evangelicals often fall into of more generally defining ourselves as sinners rather than saints, as those in constant rebellion against God rather than his permanently adopted children.

This is probably an alarm-bell moment for many. So I need to say: we must be clear on the all-pervasive reality of sin. In reaction to a world that almost denies it exists as a category and many churches that consistently downplay it, we are right to talk repeatedly about humankind's rebellion against the God who made us. Your church might actually need to be saying more on this subject rather than less. And that's because the Bible repeatedly condemns our constant attempts to replace God with idols that just allow us to worship ourselves. When we share the gospel with our non-Christian friends, they desperately need to understand that sin is our greatest problem so that they come to see the full riches of God's wonderful solution to it in the incarnation, crucifixion, resurrection and ascension of Jesus Christ.

But in other evangelical churches we need to recognize that many long-time believers still think of themselves primarily as sinners rather than forgiven children of God. The danger is that we can spend more time talking about what we've done wrong than about all that God has done to make us right in Christ. Church meetings begin with prayers of confession that—badly introduced or understood—give the impression that we are sinners crawling back to God in the hope of getting back into his good books. We don't remind each other enough that our status permanently changed when we first trusted in Jesus. That I don't ever need to crawl back into God's presence because in Jesus, I now live in his presence all of the time. A quick survey of the New Testament will reveal that believers are defined as sinners only once (1 Timothy 1:15—and Paul is clearly not embracing it as an identity).

The neglected doctrine behind all of this is, of course, that of our union with Christ: the incredible truth that I am now bound up in his identity and so share his right standing before God forever. I am one with him. Read Ephesians 1 again and see how many times that idea comes up and all the wonderful consequences that stem from that reality. We somehow need to talk about these truths, bask in them, more.

So while we need churches that don't airbrush the reality of sin from the gospel and our lives, we also need churches that enable their members to identify themselves primarily as children of God. I know that too often church meetings have encouraged me to let my sin rather than my Savior define me, and that I have left those meetings reminded more of my same-sex attraction than my new status in Christ. They have unintentionally encouraged me to spend too much time contemplating my love of some men rather than contemplating God's love for me. I need to hear a more biblically balanced message. One that does not brush my continued sin under the carpet, and that absolutely keeps encouraging me to repent of it (1 John 1:8-10), but that prevents my sin from ever defining me. For, most of all, I need reminding of who I am in Christ, to hear words like these: "You are not what you want. You are who you are. And that's defined by the Word of God."[5]

Those are the sort of words that remind me it is plausible to be a Christian who still experiences same-sex attraction. It's when I haven't been pointed to who God's Word says I am that I think I can't go on and my identity becomes bound up again in my sin: the sex that I often want with some men.

Christ-Esteem

Our churches (including the ones I serve) need to take up the challenge posed here by Mark Yarhouse:

What the church can help people with—regardless of whether orientation changes—is identity. We can recognize that a gay script is compelling to those who struggle with same-sex attraction, especially when they see few options emerging from their community of faith. Therefore we can help develop alternative scripts that are anchored in biblical truth and centered in the person and work of Christ. We can also look at our own lives and whether we are really prepared to live in a way that makes Christ our primary identity, whether we experience same-sex attraction or not.[6]

If the primary identity that all our churches commended to all our church members was our shared identity in Christ, that would do more to defeat the plausibility problem we all face than almost anything else.

So how do you most tend to define or describe yourself? As a mom or dad, someone married or single, an accountant or artist, a success or failure, gay or straight? You need to start seeing yourself primarily as God sees you—letting him define and describe you instead. And how does he do that?

Your Creator and Redeemer God says you're his perfect child (Ephesians 1:4-5), Jesus' holy sibling (Hebrews 2:11), one of his heirs (Galatians 4:7), precious and loved by him (Isaiah 43:4), his image-bearer (Genesis 1:27). I read one of these verses at the beginning of each day to boost what I call my "Christ-esteem"—to remind myself of all I now am, united to Jesus, the perfect image of God. To ground my self-identity in him.

And at the church where I serve as pastor, we're seeking to help one another do this, making sure that our meetings together always boost our "Christ-esteem." We'll sometimes start with a Bible verse that reminds us of our new identity in Christ, we choose songs that enable us to rejoice in our permanent status in God's family, we confess our sins, remembering that they amazingly haven't stopped God's love for us in Christ—we do anything, everything, that will root our identity in who God's Word says we now are in Jesus. As a result, I leave reminded more of my new status in Christ than my same-sex attraction.

Application Question

How can we all ensure our identities are defined by God's Word and not by the world around us?

MISSTEP #2

"A family is mom, dad and 2.4 children."

The real tragedy from one family member's point of view is that I'll never have children. She wants me to find a nice man and somehow (despite the biological challenges) have my own. She sweetly thinks I'll make a good dad and that it will be appalling if that opportunity passes me by.

And, to be honest, I would love kids. I would like to get them the Playmobil pirate ship my parents didn't ever get me (despite many hints). I want to read *The Cat in the Hat* with my own child as my mom and dad did with me. I have longed to weep my way through the end of *Mary Poppins* with my own daughter or son sitting beside me.

Many other friends just want me to have someone to come home to. They don't like the fact that at the end of a busy day, they all come home to loved ones and I head back to an empty house. Some keep saying that they hope I'll meet someone nice soon. They clearly hope (and some pray) that I'll grow out of this rather irrational and damaging opposition to the prospect of a nice permanent, faithful, stable gay relationship sometime soon.

And, of course, I would love to come home and be embraced. I try not to think too much about the possibility of being able to sit down and talk about the day with someone who is a permanent part of my daily life. I think people sometimes presume that I wouldn't like that—but of course I would. I long for it all the time. I want, I need, a happy family—just as many other people do who are single for a whole host of different reasons.

But I do have a family! Not just my wonderful parents, siblings, nephews (one of whom I've bought that pirate ship for), nieces, in-laws, aunts, uncles, cousins—scattered throughout the UK and wider world, but a real family here in Bristol too. And not some scandalous partner and children that I've been keeping hidden in a cupboard, but members of my church—Emmanuel Church, Bristol.

Really? Isn't talk of church as family just a bit of good PR to try to make it feel like something it never really is? A rather lame attempt to make single church members feel a little bit better as they sit alone surrounded by hordes of young families, all with numerous children named after the Minor Prophets? No! It's an idea that comes from Jesus himself:

> While Jesus was still talking to the crowd, his mother and brothers stood outside, wanting to speak to him. Someone told him, "Your mother and brothers are standing outside, wanting to speak to you."
>
> He replied to him, "Who is my mother, and who are my brothers?" Pointing to his disciples, he said, "Here are my mother and my brothers. For whoever does the will of my Father in heaven is my brother and sister and mother." (Matthew 12:46-50)

It turns out that Jesus defines his family as those who follow him rather than those who are related to him. This didn't mean that his immediate family didn't matter to him. After all, he made sure his mother was going to be looked after even as he died on the cross. But it shows that talk of church family isn't just a PR stunt—it's a spiritual reality.

It was Jesus himself who first used family language to describe his initial followers, the group that became the Christian church. The rest of the New Testament follows his lead by consistently using family language to describe both what the church is, and how it should function (read Paul's first letter to Timothy for numerous examples). One of the most radical changes between the two Testaments seems to be that the biological family matters much less than it used to. In the Old Testament, having a wife and children was seen as a sign of God's blessing (see Psalm 128). In the New Testament, it's noticeable that the stress is now on growing the church rather than your own biological family; its two dominant figures—Jesus and Paul—were both single.

Happy Church Families?

The problem is that in many evangelical churches today, you might end up thinking that the Great Commission (Matthew 28:18-20) was all about going and making babies. Obviously that is one way of making disciples (although not always the most effective), but it is not the only way. The apostle Paul clearly felt he had children throughout the world, despite having had none of his own. He sees Timothy, whom he'd mentored, as his "dear son" (2 Timothy 1:2) and felt parental toward whole churches too (1 Thessalonians 2:1-12). The churches he'd planted were his children, his real family—despite the fact that he was a single man.

But this reality has been lost in many of our churches. We pay lip service to the family language, but the experience is gone.

Moms, dads and their 2.4 children tend to settle in quickly, but you can arrive as a single parent, a divorcee, a widow or widower, a single man or woman for whatever reason, and find that people don't know what to do with you—unless you are in your twenties and can join the singles group (and get married quick). The impression that we unintentionally give is that the church is made up of biological families, and that unless you are part of one of these conveniently shaped building blocks, you won't ever fit in.

And the pressures that these families put themselves under mean that they have very little time to look beyond their own borders. Many have shared this with me and it's not hard to sympathize. Responsibly they are working hard to provide for their families—often both parents working long hours to pay for their home in the leafy suburbs. Rightly concerned about marital breakdown, they make it a priority to have a weekly date night. Understandably wanting the best for their children, they rush around most evenings and weekends, carting Hosea and Obadiah between after-school clubs, music lessons, math tutors, soccer matches and parties. They are so busy keeping their own family going they don't really have time to interact with others—unless, perhaps, they have children who will play well with their own.

So if you have a family, you can reasonably feel you have time for no one else. But that can mean that unless you have a family, you feel you have no one at all. And that does not make the single life feel plausible to anyone—most of all for the biblically faithful, same-sex attracted Christians who don't even have the hope of having their own families at some stage. Listen to one of us describe how painful this can be:

> Of course you can be preoccupied for a good deal of the time with your work, and find it really does take your mind

off yourself. Even so you can hardly help but have some leisure; and what is to fill that? Well, a whole heap of interests, to keep your time and your hands and your thoughts busy, yes, and your emotions too. But what then? You come home to yourself again: the embers are cold in the grate, and the house is empty.[1]

It can be an incredibly lonely life. Unless, that is, we take Jesus' definition of family and really *live* it. Unless we notice Paul's experience of family and work together to copy it. Unless we wake up to the radical New Testament idea that church really is family—and that Mom, Dad and 2.4 children as the only family is just an unhealthy, late-twentieth-century construct. After all, before that, most people lived in larger, intergenerational family groups. Thankfully, many are already grasping this. Pastor John Piper is just one:

> Marriage and family are temporary for this age; the church is forever. I am declaring the radical biblical truth that being in a human family is no sign of eternal blessing, but being in God's family means being eternally blessed. Relationships based on family are temporary. Relationships based on union with Christ are eternal. Marriage is a temporary institution, but what it stands for lasts forever.[2]

Fortunately (and I know this can be rare), I'm part of a church that is working hard to grasp all of this for ourselves. We're not there yet, but we are, I think, beginning to make some progress. So I do feel part of a family. I *am* part of a family. Let me illustrate.

My Church Family

I arrive at church meetings and hug my honorary aunt Ruth (who's just turned seventy). She's single too, and we've talked about how we both miss physical affection—and so now in this way we provide some for each other.

On a Tuesday evening, I drop in on a family who lives just around the corner, overexcite Charlie and Toby (the latter being one of my twelve godchildren) just before bedtime, and then have supper with their patient parents, Jim and Claire. I love sitting down and talking life and ministry with them (Jim is one of my fellow pastors).

Midweek, I try to meet up with a group of church friends in a local café and catch up on the week. We're often a mix of single people and some married couples—it works best when there's a cross section of people there so that there are more life experiences (and pizza) to share.

On a Thursday night, Jack often pops in on his way back from work and we put the world right from a single man's perspective. I've known him since he was a young Christian and student and have had the pleasure of helping and watching him grow into a mature Christian who pours himself into serving Jesus at work and church—and further afield.

On Sundays, in the time between our church meeting and small group, I go out for coffee with a couple and their two daughters. I've known Simon and Lucy for over ten years and was the best man at their wedding. We depend on each other for advice; we know about each others' families, finances and faith. I'm godfather to Katie (and have read *The Cat in the Hat* to her), and I've been chosen as a potential legal guardian to both her and her sister Hannah.

Another couple invites me to travel with them and opens up their home all the time. David and Jolsna have cooked about four hundred meals for me at the last count—and I cried through the end of *Mary Poppins* with their daughter Malati. Paul and Jo are often there and have me over for meals too; David, Jolsna and I share their son Jacob as a godchild.

I hadn't gotten around to making any plans for my last birthday, so the couple I lead a small group with, Paul and Helen, organized a party. Fifty church family members came with just two days' notice.

John and Avril are my parents' age but have become some of my closest friends—although John's skill and speed at Scrabble has tested that friendship at times. We enjoy the same TV series—like *West Wing* and *M*A*S*H*—and *some* of the same music, such as James Taylor.

I could go on and talk about Tim and Ali, Jay and Rosie, Phil and others. I have people I can call—and who call me—at 10 p.m. so that there's someone to talk to when I get in after a long day. They know that I often find this time hard and have offered to help.

Last time I was sick, I needed a receptionist to help me cope with all the offers of help. My freezer is still stocked up with the soups and casseroles that people brought me.

God has very kindly put me in a family of people of all ages, backgrounds and circumstances, and we are slowly learning to be family to one another—as Jesus says we should be, as Jesus has made us to be. He was, as ever, telling us the truth when he said,

> "Truly I tell you," Jesus replied, "no one who has left home or brothers or sisters or mother or father or children or fields for me and the gospel will fail to receive a hundred times as much in this present age: homes, brothers, sisters, mothers, children and fields—along with persecutions— and in the age to come eternal life." (Mark 10:29-30)

And, crucially, this new family benefits us all—there is give and take from all of us, all of the time. It strengthens single people, but it also strengthens marriages. It allows children to grow up in an environment where there are multiple adults parenting them. It's not perfect—there are constant ups and downs. All human relationships get messy at times, but they are a mess worth making. Because when it works, it is the most wonderful of experiences for all of us. I pinch myself at times.

And the plausibility of the life that I have chosen is closely tied to this experience. When church feels like a family, I can cope with not ever having my own partner and children. When it hasn't worked is when I have struggled most. The same-sex attracted Christians I've met who are suffering most are those in churches that haven't grasped this at all and that don't even notice these individuals.

Your Church Family

So, do you want to help make biblical teaching on homosexuality seem reasonable? Do you want to help tackle the plausibility problem? Then start acting out the Christian reality that family equals church, whatever life circumstance God has put you in. Recognize the misstep that family is Mom, Dad and 2.4 children. It will help others (and you) more than you know.

Start by talking to people of different ages and life situations to find out what they most need and appreciate. It might be as simple as doing some of the things that my church members very kindly do for me, or it might be different.

One single friend of mine finds times with families a painful reminder of what she's never had but really appreciates meals out with her married female friends on their own (who themselves love the excuse for an evening away from their children and husbands). Another single friend helps himself (and others) by regularly organizing mountain biking trips that mix singles and marrieds. Do your research!

But don't just talk. *Do* something. Don't wait for others to make this happen. If you wait, almost certainly nothing will happen. So who in your church family are you going to invite to see that film with you on Wednesday night? Who could share that midweek meal that you'd otherwise be eating alone? Does your summer break give you a chance to organize a vacation that will get a group of families and single people going away together? Acting like a church family doesn't necessarily add a whole host of new things to the "to-do list"; it just means involving your brothers and sisters in Christ in what you were planning on doing anyway. And *you* can take the initiative in doing this, whether you're married or single. What could you do *today*?

Application Question

How can we all make sure that talk of "church family" isn't just talk?

"If you're born gay, it can't be wrong to be gay."

How can being gay be wrong *if you were born gay?* That's a question I'm asked a lot. And it's a good one: my same-sex attraction feels part of me in that sort of way. As a theory on the origins of homosexuality, being born gay works for me better than any of the others on the market today, although every same-sex attracted man or woman will, no doubt, have their own personal take on this most complex and controversial area. As I've interacted with a whole range of same-sex attracted people, I keep being struck by how unique everyone's sexuality is in both its development and expression. This is not an area for generalizations or dogmatism.

But back to me! Personally, being born gay is more convincing to me than the idea that I one day woke up and consciously chose to be attracted to some men. In reality, as puberty began, I was as instinctively drawn to some of the boys I was growing up with as they were instinctively drawn to some of the girls. I simply felt wired differently. I carried out no rewiring myself. Although there is evidence supporting the fluidity of sexuality in some people (especially women), there is little scientific evidence that we ourselves can simply turn our own desires on and off by an act of our will (although we can, of course, choose to intensify them).

But, according to others, I don't have to accept the responsibility myself. Any fault lies with my parents: I can, if I want to, blame them. My close relationship with my domineering mother and my broken relationship with my passive father shaped my sexuality from an early age. Except that my mom and dad don't fit those crude stereotypes at all. They'd be the first to say that they aren't perfect, but I've enjoyed a good relationship with them both throughout my life. Tragically, one of the things that most stopped me from being more open about my sexuality was my fear that they'd be blamed for it by others.

Being sexually abused as a child is what really caused it—being seduced as a young teenager by that older man so damaged my sexuality that I've ended up with same-sex attraction. That's another theory on the market. But that never happened to me. No adult ever laid a finger on me like that. My sexuality has not been shaped in this way by anyone else.

My lack of hand-to-eye coordination is another potential guilty party, according to some. Not being able to catch a ball, always being one of the last chosen for sports teams, shaped me into someone who sexually desired the sort of man I would never be. My lack of binocular vision is to blame! But many friends had the same experience as children and are entirely heterosexual. Would I really change if I became good at football? That has been suggested! But I still can't see a football properly.

So It's in My Genes?

Cue talk of the "gay gene"—the claim that same-sex attraction is there in my DNA. I was born with auburn hair. I was born gay.

There is nothing I can do about either (except the auburn hair is fading while the same-sex attraction is not).

And if that's the case, say many, my same-sex attraction is natural and so it can't be wrong to express it sexually. If it's genetic, it must be right. Indeed it would be a crime to say that I can't—a denial of my human right to be myself.

I hope you feel the power of this argument—whether you agree with the "gay gene" theory or not. It is certainly the one that fits best with my lived experience of same-sex attraction (if not everyone's). It is the most powerful case for affirming homosexuality today. And, I guess, that's why some evangelical Christians have put a huge amount of time and energy into fighting the idea that same-sex attraction is genetic or innate. The scientific evidence for and against has become one of the most fought-over pieces of ground in this whole debate—rather like a patch of grass in the middle of no-man's land at the height of the First World War.

But I think we could afford to concede this ground. Now, the scientific case for doing so is admittedly poor. Despite some hyped-up newspaper headlines, a "gay gene" has yet to be found—indeed, the evidence for it has actually weakened over the last couple of decades. In her recent book *Straight Expectations*, gay journalist Julie Bindel asks geneticist Dr. Andrew Rutherford whether it actually exists. He replies, "I feel I can give you an unequivocal answer to that question, which also applies to the biology of almost any complex trait, which is, there isn't a gay gene."[1]

But, I want to argue, even if the "gay gene" were found tomorrow, we would still not need to worry about this particular battle being lost: a genetic basis for homosexuality would not make it right; it would not equal a lack of responsibility and thus open the floodgates to liberalism. Indeed, it has been a significant and damaging theological misstep for people in the church to think that this would be so.

You see, one of the central truths of the Bible is that we are all naturally sinners from birth and yet are still held responsible for our sin. And so being born same-sex attracted, and yet being reproached for acting on it, is not a problem in its pages. Since the fall, the Bible maintains that sin infects every part of us because we have a sinful genetic inheritance (manifested in countless different ways). And yet one of the glories of being human, created in the image of God, is being treated by our Creator God as responsible for what we think, say and do.

Original Sin

What we're talking about here is what theologians call the doctrine of original sin. And one of the places where it's articulated best is in Psalm 51. It's the psalm composed by the Old Testament King David after he'd committed adultery with Bathsheba and had her husband Uriah killed to cover his tracks (see 2 Samuel 11–12 for all the sordid details). In the psalm, he says this:

> Surely I was sinful at birth,
>   sinful from the time my mother conceived me.
>   (Psalm 51:5)

Here King David recognizes in himself what we have just been saying is true of all human beings—we are all born with an inbuilt instinct to sin. It comes naturally to us.

In today's world, we'd expect David to go on to use that reality to excuse his adultery and murder. To explain it away as not really his fault, to be part of a justification for his crimes on the basis that "I was born sexually promiscuous. You can't make me re-

sponsible for something I was born with a natural instinct to do."
But those are not the words he uses in this context. Psalm 51 is
all about King David taking responsibility for his actions. This is
what he says to God just before his words above:

> For I know my transgressions,
>   and my sin is always before me.
> Against you, you only, have I sinned
>   and done what is evil in your sight;
> so you are right in your verdict
>   and justified when you judge. (Psalm 51:3-4)

And this is what he says just a little bit later:

> Cleanse me with hyssop, and I will be clean;
>   wash me, and I will be whiter than snow.
> Let me hear joy and gladness;
>   let the bones you have crushed rejoice.
> Hide your face from my sins
>   and blot out all my iniquity. (Psalm 51:7-9)

He's taking full responsibility—even as he notes his natural tendency to behave in this way. King David believes he was born a
sinner and yet still regards himself as completely responsible
for his sin.

And his point is made again and again through Scripture. King
David is not a biblical eccentric. "Why haven't I heard about
original sin before?" might be the question you're asking. Well, like
quite a bit of the Bible's teaching, it sounds a bit unfair to us at first.
That means people don't like it, so preachers and teachers tend to
keep quiet about it. As English professor Alan Jacobs has put it:

> We struggle to hold together a model of human sinfulness
> that is universal rather than local, in which we inherit sin

rather than choose it, and in which, nevertheless, we are fully, terrifyingly responsible for our condition.[2]

And yet, as Jacobs points out in his book on the subject (written because it's an idea that dominates so much of the English literary canon), "the individual components of the idea are utterly familiar."[3] We all know it's a sad reality of life that

> some people are born with a malady of some kind: a birth defect resulting from the mistransmission of genetic information, say, or a disorder (HIV, hepatitis) passed from mother to child through the umbilical cord.[4]

However, we also constantly recognize that our inherited problems are not just medical but also moral. We each inherit patterns of sin. Just think for a moment of regularly heard comments like "He has his father's temper," or "The Smith family has a long history of alcohol problems." I've inherited a stubbornness that my mother stubbornly maintains comes from my father's side of the family.

And yet, despite the fact that we were all born with a tendency to behave in certain ways and that we have perhaps a familial spin on sin, we do still hold each other responsible for our attitudes and actions. Inherited bad traits might increase our empathy for someone as they struggle to overcome them, but that doesn't make them right or unpunishable. We'd instinctively recognize that if someone we loved were murdered by an angry drunk. Or if you ever had to deal with me in a particularly stubborn mood.

Most of us already adhere to the individual ideas that make up the doctrine of original sin (and what flows from it): that we were born imperfect into an imperfect world, and yet can and should be held to account for our imperfections. It is just that we have failed to connect the dots in the way that the Bible helpfully does and to label those imperfections as God does—as original sin, our inbuilt tendency to rebel instinctively in particular ways against the God who made us. We see the various results, but unlike God through his Word, we don't state the cause with clarity.

Are you with me so far? This is one of the hardest things I have to explain in this book, but it is important to get your mind around it. The Bible teaches, and life around us shows, that we are all born with an innate ability and desire to sin. We can't help ourselves. And yet, the Bible clearly states that we are held responsible for our sins.

Same-Sex Attraction and Original Sin

Back to same-sex attraction. Back to the question I opened this chapter with: How can being same-sex attracted be wrong if you were born gay? Very easily, in the light of this Bible teaching—I was not born perfect (just ask my mother about my stubbornness!). I was born with loads of other things wrong with me, some of them unique to me. One of these things was the beginnings of a uniquely flawed sexuality (everyone's is flawed differently and develops in different ways), which might well be the chief determining factor in the sexual attraction I now feel toward certain men. But potentially being born "gay" (as it is crudely put) does not necessarily make it right for me to embrace a gay identity and lifestyle. New Testament expert Richard Hays makes this point well:

> The very nature of sin is that it is *not* freely chosen. That
> is what it means to live "in the flesh" in a fallen creation.

> We are in bondage to sin but still held accountable to
> God's righteous judgment of our actions. In the light of
> this theological anthropology, it cannot be maintained
> that a homosexual orientation is morally neutral because
> it is involuntary.[5]

I was born with no choice about whether to sin or not. And yet
sin is still wrong. And I am responsible to God for it. I could
have been born same-sex attracted—it can feel totally instinctive
to me—but I am still held responsible for acting on it.

Our knowledge of what is right and wrong cannot be derived
from what comes naturally to us because everything that is
wrong with this world came naturally from us. Morality has to
be defined by someone outside of us. And it is—by the God who
created us.

So, to many in the Christian church, we need to say: of all the
people on the planet, we should be those most comfortable with
people being born gay (if that's really the case), and yet still think
it wrong to express that sexually. It's been a massive misstep not
to articulate this.

And we need to stop being afraid of the lived experience of
many same-sex attracted people—that they have always felt this
way. We have done many of them a disservice by refusing to
accept this in the past—not just because of the damage it's
caused them but because of the damage it's done to the doctrine
of original sin. Our misstep has been bad for us all.

For you too were born with no choice about whether to sin or
not. And yet that sin is still wrong. And you too are responsible
to God for it—whatever form it might have taken in your life.
You were born with an inbuilt tendency to sin in a particular way.
It felt totally instinctive to you, and yet you will still be held

responsible for acting on it. And you need to know that in order to help you make sense of yourself and your struggle with sin.

People around us will only make sense of what it means to be human if they join us in taking seriously this key doctrine and all that springs from it. We all need to stop trusting in ourselves and our natural instincts. They have got us into the mess we're in, in so many different contexts. Following our natural instincts has ruined the environment, relationships, economies and everything else—it is past time we turned our attention to the God who more accurately determines what is right and wrong for our lasting benefit.

Application Question

How can we better communicate that a natural instinct to do something doesn't mean it must be right?

MISSTEP #4

"If it makes you happy, it must be right!"

I have what I call "kitchen floor moments." I call them that because they involve me sitting on my kitchen floor. But I'm not doing something useful like scrubbing it, although it could always benefit from that. Instead I'm there crying. And the reason for my tears is the unhappiness that my experience of same-sex attraction often brings. The acute pain I sometimes feel as a result of not having a partner, sex, children and the rest.

I know what my non-Christian friends and family would say to me in these moments. If not acting on my same-sex attraction makes me so unhappy, I should start acting on it. I should get myself a nice man, have great sex, adopt some lovely children and be happy.

I know that many of my Christian friends and family would struggle to know what to say to me in these moments. My unhappiness in not acting on my same-sex attraction is what most persuades them that I should act on it. Surely God wants us to be happy. If I could find myself a nice Christian man and "marry" him, what could be wrong with me having sex and children with him? How can God condemn something that would bring such happiness to so many people?

Why do I arrogantly think I know what most people would say? Because that's where my mind goes too—because *the* great authority in the world we live in today is our personal happiness. If someone or something leads to unhappiness in our life, they or it must be wrong. If someone or something makes us happy, they or it must be right.

The evidence for this is everywhere. Happiness is what the commercials promise us if we buy their product. It's what the politicians will deliver us if we give them our vote. It's what the new love of our life offers us if we ditch the old. It's why human beings today do most things. We just want to be happy, and all our decisions are driven by what will get us the most happiness soonest (and, perhaps, cheapest).

But surely this isn't true of the evangelical church! We spend a lot of our time pointing all this out—alerting others to the dangers. Let's see how this misstep has infiltrated our own churches, how we let our personal happiness determine our decisions too. I think just two examples will make the case for me.

Go back a few generations and you will find that divorce was not an option for most Christians. Pastors would only have recommended it in the worst cases of serial adultery or spousal abuse (and rightly so). But today it is no longer a rarity in church families. What is used to justify this? Our happiness. It can't be good to stay in a marriage that is making you unhappy. Because we're now convinced that God just wants us to be happy, we happily ignore what he says about divorce (Matthew 5:31-32).

In the same way, Western Christians' attitudes toward economic prosperity are rooted in our belief that God is 100 percent committed to our happiness—happiness defined by our society, not him. Although we'd never admit it, and regularly condemn peddlers of the "prosperity gospel," we've joined the world around us in believing that money buys happiness. So we'll give away what we can afford, but only after we've paid for what we no longer consider luxuries: the third pair of shoes, the latest phone, the overseas trip, the fees at the school with the world-class facilities, the pension that will leave our lifestyle unchanged until the day we die. Few pastors would dare ask church members to sacrifice the happiness that these things apparently guarantee. In past generations, the lifestyles of many Christians were observably different from those of their non-Christian neighbors—today, there is often nothing to tell us apart. We fear our lives would be less happy without these things. And because we presume that God wants us to be happy, we happily ignore what his Word says about the sort of generosity that gives away more than we think we can afford (2 Corinthians 8–9).

Today's ruling authority *is* our short-term happiness—both outside *and* inside the church. And we have sometimes blatantly (liberal parts of the church) and sometimes more subtly (evangelicals) changed our God to fit in with our desire to just be happy. He's now often, to borrow Tim Keller's phrase, a "Stepford God."[1] A god of our own making (like the *Stepford Wives*, created by their husbands), a god who wants us to be happy in the ways we (driven by the society around us) want to be happy. A totem pole of a god who would never contradict what we want to be able to do.

In fact, in many church contexts, the main group who are still being asked to do something that makes them unhappy are the Christians who experience same-sex attraction. And so there is an understandable (almost admirable) consistency in now allowing them to do what they want to as well. Then we can all be happy together!

Why Be Unhappy?

In an environment where happiness is nearly always *the* authority, my decision not to act on my same-sex attraction seems totally implausible because it often makes me so unhappy. I'm not just going against my own powerful desires; it feels as though I'm going against the flow of the whole world around me. So why not conclude that God just wants me to be happy and happily ignore what he says about hating homosexual sex (Leviticus 18:22)?

What stops me from reaching for the white out and applying it liberally to my Bible? Well, I am not convinced that doing what I *think* would make me happy would *actually* make me happy. If I had been able to have sex with every man I've wanted to have sex with, I would have led a sexually promiscuous life. At the time, I thought each man would make me happy. And they might have—for a time. But the pleasure would have been fleeting. Many of the consequences would have been bad for me, for them and for others too.

How do I know this? Because, at its most honest, the world around us makes this point. Some of the Hollywood films I have watched recently have powerfully made the point that sexual promiscuity does not bring happiness—quite the reverse. I've surprisingly had my wrong worldly view that lots of sex equals lots of happiness quickly corrected by non-Christian film makers.

In lots of different contexts, people in the world around us are waking up to the truth that living to make ourselves happy in the here and now is actually a sure way to guarantee unhappiness in the longer term. Back to those who get divorced at the first sign of unhappiness in a marriage—in their book on marriage, Tim and Kathy Keller help make this point by pointing to secular statistics: "Longitudinal studies demonstrate that two-thirds of those unhappy marriages out there will become happy within five years if people stay married and do not get divorced."[2] Many who have encouraged other people to leave an unhappy marriage for the sake of their happiness may have actually done them a disservice.

And take the example of materialism again. The number of non-Christians deliberately downsizing also shows that many have recognized the lie that just a few more things, one more vacation, better educational facilities and a fat pension are enough to buy you (and those you love) true happiness. We need something else to live for, to live by. The plausibility problem here actually belongs to the world around us—and many of our non-Christian friends and families are beginning to get it.

True Happiness

What we all need is a new authority. Actually, what we most need is the old authority: God himself—someone apart from ourselves to live for, someone else's rules to live by. We need to start following and listening to him.

Why? Why replace our primary desire for happiness with a primary desire to obey God's Word? Why surrender our personal sovereignty to him? I find the middle section of Psalm 19 persuasive:

> The law of the LORD is perfect,
>   refreshing the soul.
> The statutes of the LORD are trustworthy,
>   making wise the simple.
> The precepts of the LORD are right,
>   giving joy to the heart.

The commands of the LORD are radiant,
    giving light to the eyes.
The fear of the LORD is pure,
    enduring forever.
The decrees of the LORD are firm,
    and all of them are righteous.
They are more precious than gold,
    than much pure gold;
they are sweeter than honey,
    than honey from the honeycomb.
By them your servant is warned;
    in keeping them there is great reward. (Psalm 19:7-11)

The world around us is constantly changing its mind about what will bring us happiness. At some points in history true happiness has been promised through sexual faithfulness (the 1950s), but at other times only through sexual promiscuity (the 1960s). A little further back in history, Victorian sexual repression was a reaction to Georgian sexual license. A same-sex attracted man or woman born in 1930 would have spent most of their life being told by society to repress those desires—and only in the last couple of decades (when they'd reached their seventies and eighties) would they be allowed to express them freely. Who knows where we'll be told happiness is to be found in another fifty years' time? Everything will almost certainly change again completely, whether we're talking about sex or anything else. Who knows when society has gone too far in one direction or too far in another? The pendulum swings on almost every issue have been massive, and we never know in what direction we're heading at any moment.

In contrast, God's Word (his law, statutes, precepts, commands and decrees—the contents of our Bibles today) provides us with the perfect and trustworthy wisdom we need. Unsure about what is really good for you? God's Word is always right and will show you what it is good to do. In a world where all other authorities change their minds, it is permanent and sure. Its divine origin gives us the all-seeing and all-knowing timeless perspective that is a worthy authority to live our lives by. Especially, as the opening verses of Psalm 19 recall, their ultimate author is also our Creator—who knows what is best for us. That's why the psalmist says that his law is worth more than gold and tastier than honey.

And, interestingly, obey God's Word and we'll get the true happiness that we long for too. Our souls will be refreshed, wisdom will be ours, we'll experience true joy, have all the insight we need in life and be wonderfully rewarded for our obedience. These unambiguous promises in this psalm (and repeated throughout Scripture: Matthew 5:1-10; John 10:10) replace our primary desire for our personal happiness with a primary desire to obey God's Word and mean that true happiness will be ours for free.

And those are the biblical truths that stop me acting on my same-sex attraction. They have the power to keep me loyal to God's Word when obedience to his commands has left me crying on my kitchen floor. They assure me of the truth of something my favorite author of all, C. S. Lewis, once wrote:

> When we want to be something other than the thing God wants us to be, we must be wanting what, in fact, will not make us happy. Those Divine demands which sound to our natural ears most like those of a despot and least like those of a lover, in fact marshal us where we should want to go if we knew what we wanted.[3]

When I want to live life as a gay man, to embrace the whole modern identity and lifestyle, God's Word assures me that it will not make me happy—even though denying my sexual feelings the affirmation and expression I so want sounds cruel and un-loving, it is actually what I would choose myself if I knew what was best for me. Psalm 19 guarantees me what I most want, even as it stops me getting it in the way I often want it.

That's why I'm seeking to make God's Word *the* authority in my life rather that what I (or any other human being) might think will bring me happiness. Which, of course, is what being a Christian is really all about: taking God at his Word, and so trusting him. Doing the very opposite—not taking God at his Word, and so disobeying him—is what humanity has done instinctively ever since Adam and Eve led the way in Genesis 3.

At the heart of being a Christian is a recognition that we have been submitting to the wrong authority—our own hap-piness. And that we need to submit to a new authority—God's way to be happy as set out in his Word. That is why there is something deeply wrong when Christians start editing out those bits of the Bible they aren't happy with—it shows that they are not really submitting to God after all, but want to continue to define what is right and wrong for themselves. This has always been a mistake and has caused all the unhappiness in our world (Genesis 3 again). As Christians, we're meant to impersonate not the disobedience of our human parents (Adam and Eve) but the complete obedience of our Lord and Savior (Jesus Christ). He fully submitted to everything God's Word told him to, for the joy that he knew would soon be his (Hebrews 12:2). We will have the same experience if we display the same patient obedience.

Lasting Happiness

Now, that will mean some temporary unhappiness—Jesus' example should prepare us for this. But it won't mean sacrificing happiness forever. It will just postpone it—or, better put, it will exchange it for the genuine, lasting article that we'll start to experience even now. It's not just "pie in the sky when you die." For me it will probably involve some more kitchen floor moments. But what will get me up off the kitchen floor is embracing the truth that the long-term happiness I long for comes through obedience to God's Word.

What will also help me get up off the kitchen floor is seeing other Christians sacrifice short-term happiness out of obedience to God's Word. I'm most encouraged to obey what God says about sex by the costly obedience I see other Christians make in some totally different areas of their lives—due to some very different divine commands. Some of my church's mission partners have sacrificed an easy life in the UK for a hard life as student workers in Greece and Japan—out of obedience to the Great Commission. A good friend has been willing to sacrifice his professional reputation to take a stand for the truth—because of his conviction that God wants his people always to speak the truth. Another friend persevered in a marriage nearly everyone else would have walked away from—because he knows his God hates divorce. A colleague rejected a promising academic career to work for our church— because she believes that's how God is asking her to use her gifts. All of them are (probably much to their surprise) the sort of people who have most made me feel the plausibility of the life that I'm living, and I praise God for them. They've created the sort of plausibility structure I need. Without them, I'd find it much harder to get up off the kitchen floor.

So, do you want to make the life of Christians who experience same-sex attraction more plausible? Then do the same sort of counter-cultural things! Take a moment now to review the latest big decision you made: if you're honest, were your actions driven primarily by what would make you happy in the here and now? If that was the case, recognize the misstep of thinking that if it makes you happy, it must be right. Repent and stop seeing your personal happiness as the authority in your life; embrace God's Word as your authority. Experience the temporary unhappiness that this will often bring in the certain hope of the lasting happiness that God's Word promises will eventually be all yours in his new creation—forever and a day.

Application Question

How can we all keep checking that our decisions aren't more governed by what we feel than what God's Word says is good for us?

MISSTEP #5

"Sex is where true intimacy is found."

I once googled the word *intimacy* and found the images to be 99 percent sexual. In our Western world today, intimacy equals sex. Want to experience intimacy? You need to have sex. The two are nearly always inseparable in our minds.

We illustrate this in our instinctive interpretation of just one Bible verse. It records part of a lament the Old Testament King David composed on hearing of the death of his best friend, King Saul's son Jonathan. And it contains these moving words:

> I grieve for you, Jonathan my brother;
>> you were very dear to me.
> Your love for me was wonderful,
>> more wonderful than that of women. (2 Samuel 1:26)

Today it seems impossible for anyone to read this song without thinking that David and Jonathan must have enjoyed a sexual relationship. Didn't you find yourself quickly sniffing out something homoerotic about them? Off the back of this one verse, some have even claimed biblical approval of gay relationships—all because David says Jonathan's love for him was better than a woman's. We just can't stop ourselves.

But what about the more plausible theory that Jonathan's simple friendship was more precious to David than his complicated relationships with women? (First Samuel 25:42-44 lists three wives at this stage of David's life.) Why is it not possible that he enjoyed the non-sexual intimacy of his friendship with Jonathan (also a married man) more than the sexual intimacy of his relationships with Abigail, Ahinoam and Michal? Why not conclude that he's not saying Jonathan was better in bed than his wives—but that Jonathan's friendship was better than anything David did in bed with his wives?

Sadly, we don't seem to be able to conceive of that possibility today. Such intimacy must mean sex. Our sex lives are meant to be the best things about our lives. But I think that tells us more about our relationships today than David and Jonathan's back then. We live in a society whose only route to true intimacy has become the joy of sex.

And the consequences for someone like me sound pretty tragic: no intimate relationships because I'm saying no to sex. My life will thus be a lonely one without the sort of relationships that any human being needs to survive, let alone thrive. No wonder so many think the celibate life I've chosen just isn't plausible—that I'll either wither away slowly or (preferably) give up on it very soon.

Intimacy Matters

Human beings need intimacy. Without it we die inside—even if we might keep going through the motions on the outside. God himself speaks clearly of this need (Genesis 2:18). Church minister Kate Wharton helpfully fleshes this out:

> Ever since God declared that it was "not good" for Adam to be alone, human beings have been living alongside one

another, sharing life together. I need other people in my life. I need them to offload to after a bad day; I need them to work alongside me in ministry; I need them to share a bottle of wine with me as we put the world to rights; I need them to point out to me the parts of my character that need working on; I need them to celebrate with me when good things happen; I need them to spend my days off and holidays with; I need them to give me a hug and tell me everything's going to be OK.[1]

I need intimacy in all these ways. So I need to be in an intimate sexual relationship, to have "someone special." That would seem to be the point that she's making. But it's not. She's a single woman (not same-sex attracted—just for the record) who is talking about the God-given need for us all to live our lives in community. She's making the much-ignored point that God's answer to the problem of human loneliness is not just the sexual intimacy of marriage, but everything that first marriage made possible. From it came more people and the possibility of life in community. In denying me a sexual partner, God is not denying me intimate relationships—he provides them in countless other ways.

So, interestingly, I don't feel it is God who is preventing me from having intimate relationships. Instead, they are often closed off to me by our society and sexualized culture. The world in which we live cannot cope with intimate relationships that aren't sexual—it makes no sense; it's just not possible. So I've had to pull back from deepening friendships with both men and women out of fear that they are being seen as inappropriate. None of them were—but the supposed impossibility of nonsexual intimacy meant we felt under pressure to close them down. That's been very hard at times.

But what's been hardest is how the church often discourages non-sexual intimacy too. Our response to the sexual revolution going on outside our doors has sadly just been to promote sexual intimacy in the context of Christian marriage. And to encourage people to keep it there by promising this will then deliver all the intimacy they've ever wanted. Journalist Andrew Sullivan makes this point:

> The Christian churches, which once . . . held out the virtue of friendship as equal to the benefit of conjugal love, are our culture's primary and obsessive propagandists for the marital unit and its capacity to resolve all human ills and satisfy all human needs.[2]

I wish I could say this wasn't true. But it is! If our churches put as much time and energy into promoting good friendships as they do good marriages, life would be much easier for people like me. And, interestingly, much better for everyone else too. Sullivan goes on to point out a tragic consequence of this Christian idolatry of marriage:

> Families and marriages fail too often because they are trying to answer too many human needs. A spouse is required to be a lover, a friend, a mother, a father, a soul mate, a co-worker, and so on. Few people can be all these things for one person. And when demands are set too high, disappointment can only follow. If husbands and wives have deeper and stronger friendships outside the marital unit, the marriage has more space to breathe and fewer burdens to bear.[3]

We need to read the whole of our Bibles again. In them, we will keep finding passages that urge us to promote and protect marriage (in just the book of Proverbs: 5; 7; 21:9), but we will also keep discovering (perhaps for the first time) a surprising number of passages that urge us to promote and protect friendships too (Proverbs 17:17; 18:24; 27:5-6, 9-10). We need to start doing both—not only so that people like me survive and thrive, but so that our marriages and families do too.

Intimate Friendships

And this will only happen if we aim at intimacy in friendships as well as in marriage. Intimate friendships are what make my life possible today. I have a number of relationships with people who know me very well. They know most things about me—the good, the bad and the ugly. And they love and care for me, despite that knowledge, and I return the compliment, despite the similar knowledge I have about them.

Phil and Caroline are two single friends that I drink gin and champagne with—though not at the same time! They laugh with me and at me (an excellent combination) and are two of the people with whom I most like to spend time. I go on vacation with them each year along with a whole group of other friends who have shared our lives with one another for a good decade or more. It's a beautiful thing.

To take another sample, let me tell you about my friendship with Julian, Mark, Matthew and Neil. We met at a Bible college. We always sat together in the same part of the lecture room. We gradually got to know each other. Off the back of a scary talk about all the ways in which we could shipwreck our lives and ministries, we formed an accountability group with the aim of keeping each other walking Jesus' narrow way. We knew each other quite superficially before that talk—thirteen years later, we know each other very well.

And that has meant getting to know each other intimately.

Intentionally sharing the details of our lives that we'd rather have kept private but that have really benefited from seeing the light of day in good Christian company. I was first open and honest about my sexuality with this group of friends. They'd built up a good track record of being trustworthy people you could share hard things with—mainly by sharing the hard things they were going through themselves. Intimacy breeds intimacy—just being open and honest with other human beings encourages everyone to keep on sharing and caring. They are, as a result, the people whom God has most used to keep me going as a Christian. I couldn't be more grateful to him for them.

In a slight aside, it is interesting to note that Christian psychologist William Struthers sees this sort of godly male intimacy as the main answer to the current epidemic of pornography addiction among male church members. His is a persuasive theory:

> The myths of masculinity in our culture have isolated men from each other and impaired their ability to honor and bless one another. Too many men have too few intimate friends. Their friendships run only as deep as the things they do together. By finding male friends to go deeper with, the need for intimacy can be met in nonsexual ways with these male friends. When this happens the intensity of the need for intimacy is not funneled through sexual intercourse with a woman; it can be shared across many relationships. Sexual intimacy may be experienced with one woman, but intimacy can be experienced with others as well. Not all intimacy is genital, so do not feel restricted in your relationships with your brothers in Christ.[4]

His point is an interesting one: our sex drives are not just lessened by sexual intimacy; they can be satisfied by non-sexual intimacy, by friendship too.

My personal experience is that the power of sexual temptation lessens the more time I spend among friends with whom I am non-sexually intimate. That might sound weird, but I think it just proves the point that true intimacy is found not just in sex but also in friendships, so I'm don't have to live life without that intimacy just because I'm not getting any sex. For me, that has involved intentionally making sure my friendships with members of both sexes are more and more appropriately intimate. For other same-sex attracted people, I know that intimacy in friendships with their own sex can lead to more sexual temptation, but with honesty and accountability in place, there is no need for them to be totally avoided.

So, do you want to do your own part to tackle the plausibility problem? Work on making your friendships more intimate. I'll hazard a guess that this will be quite a challenge. We are far too used to them remaining very superficial (especially if we're men). Biblical counselor Paul David Tripp is on the money when he writes:

> We live in interwoven networks of terminally casual relationships. We live with the delusion that we know one another, but we really don't. We call our easygoing, self-protective, and often theologically platitudinous conversations "fellowship," but they seldom ever reach the threshold of true fellowship. We know cold demographic details about one another (married or single, type of job, number of kids, general location of housing, etc.), but we know little about the struggle of faith that is waged every day behind well-maintained personal boundaries.

One of the things that still shocks me in counseling, even after all these years, is how little I often know about people I have counted as true friends. I can't tell you how many times, in talking with friends who have come to me for help, that I have been hit with details of difficulty and struggle far beyond anything I would have predicted. Privatism is not just practiced by the lonely unbeliever; it is rampant in the Church as well.[5]

If, instead, we all started living in interwoven networks of increasingly intimate relationships, all of our lives would be much better.

Intimacy Creation

But how can we do that? How can we begin to construct these much-needed networks?

First of all, we need to make time for people. Friendships are built not through snatched conversations before and after church but when we linger in each other's company. So what activities do we linger over? Well (delete as appropriate): cooking, eating, drinking, washing up, watching TV, taking the kids to the playground, DIY and window-shopping all immediately spring to mind. Start inviting people to do these things with you (you'll probably be doing most of them anyway)—you'll soon get to know those people better.

Second, begin to share some intimacies with your friends. Trust them with your worries, doubts, fears and pain; ask them questions about their own. One of my best friendships was founded on just one afternoon's conversation when he asked me a few good questions. Others have developed slowly over years as we've honestly shared the ups and downs of life together.

Third, persevere! I love Anne Lamott's observation: "Rubble is the ground on which our deepest friendships are built."[6] I keep getting friendships wrong and am tempted to run away whenever I've made a mess of them once again. But my best friendships are the ones that have imploded—but then been slowly rebuilt. Friendships so often really get going after the first argument or misunderstanding and the careful, painful conversations that follow.

Want some more help with your friendships? My friend Vaughan Roberts has recently written a short book on friendship that would be the best place to turn.[7] We've recently encouraged our whole church family to read it. In it, he honestly shares his own realization of the superficiality of many of his friendships and what he did to change this—based on what the Bible says about the importance of intimate friendships. Why not read it after this book?

Application Question

How can we all develop more intimate friendships?

MISSTEP #6

"Men and women are equal and interchangeable."

What's wrong with the statement above? Take just the first part of it: Surely it's self-evident in today's world that men and women are born equal? As the writer Dorothy Sayers put it, "The fundamental thing is that women are more like men than anything else in the world. They are human beings."[1]

She was rightly correcting a society in which differences between the sexes were often overstressed to preserve supposed male superiority and dominance. But now, thanks to the battles that she and others fought, the equality of women and men is enshrined in law and increasingly, but far from perfectly, reflected in everyday life (at least in the West).

All Christians should rejoice in this equality and its biblical roots. Genesis 1 is crystal clear on this issue—it has a strong claim to be the first feminist text:

So God created mankind in his own image,
    in the image of God he created them;
    male and female he created them. (Genesis 1:27)

Men and women are fundamentally the same in the divinely bestowed dignity that sets them far above the rest of creation. They share an ability to relate to God and the job of ruling creation for him. So any belief or behavior based on the idea that men and women are different in status undermines the foundations on which humanity is built. God's Word here says we are equal—it is the first word on the subject and should be treated as the last.

And when God's Word was made flesh, we see what that equality looks like in practice—in how Jesus treated women and men as equal throughout his ministry on earth. I love Sayers's description of how Christ behaved toward women:

> It is no wonder that the women were first at the Cradle and last at the Cross. They had never known a man like this Man—there never has been such another. A prophet and teacher who never nagged at them, never flattered or coaxed or patronised; who never made arch jokes about them, never treated them either as "The women, God help us!" or "The ladies, God bless them!"; who rebuked without querulousness and praised without condescension; who took their questions and arguments seriously; who never mapped out their sphere for them, never urged them to be feminine or jeered at them for being female; who had no axe to grind and no uneasy male dignity to defend; who took them as he found them and was completely unself-conscious. There is no act, no sermon, no parable in the whole Gospel that borrows its pungency from female perversity; nobody could possibly guess from the words and deeds of Jesus that there was anything "funny" about woman's nature.[2]

You pick up a lifetime's frustration with ungodly male behavior there, wonderfully contrasted with her experience of the one perfect man, Jesus Christ. He treated women as equal to him in his perfect expression of humanity.

And the apostle Paul was also clear on this point—in both theory and practice. So there is his much-quoted declaration in Galatians: "There is neither Jew nor Gentile, neither slave nor free, nor is there male and female, for you are all one in Christ Jesus" (Galatians 3:28). But there are also his much-maligned household codes (see Ephesians 5:22-33 and Colossians 3:18-25), which counterculturally insisted on husbands treating their wives like themselves—as equal in dignity to men. The Bible consistently sees men and women as sharing the same status.

And so the church needs to repent of times when it has undermined the clarity of the biblical witness on this. To its shame there have been centuries when all this teaching was often ignored in both theory and practice—to the detriment of generations of women. We have a murky past here. And, horribly, often a murky present too: I worry that the male behavior that Sayers contrasts with Jesus' is still to be found in many evangelical churches today, as well as the world around us.

Gender Difference

So men and women are equal. This first part of the statement should be incontrovertible. But it ends badly: in righting the unbiblical wrong of not treating men and women equally, the church has made a disastrous misstep when we've insisted that the sexes are interchangeable. It's another misstep we've made encouraged by the world around us. Increasingly, our society is seeing sexual difference as irrelevant, and men and women as the same. It doesn't matter if you have two men in bed together, two women married to each other, same-sex parents—because what is there to differentiate between men and women? If men and women are exactly the same, any combination works and traditional distinctions must be thrown out.

But a binary distinction was made right back in the beginning by the God who made us all. Gender is not a social construct, it's a divine one. Let's return to Genesis 1:

> So God created mankind in his own image,
>> in the image of God he created them;
>> male and female he created them. (Genesis 1:27)

We weren't created *exactly* the same—we were created male and female. Humanity is not unisex, but made up of two different sexes. The Bible tells us that there is genuine difference at the same time as introducing the total equality of men and women.

So what are the differences? We need to tread carefully here. For every difference I mention, you will instantly think of the exception; we are inevitably dealing with generalizations at this stage. And there are some genuine socially constructed differences (supposed preferences for pink or blue), which are not our focus here. But there are obvious, observable physical differences too: the differences we regularly use to work out whether someone's male or female, those that are often the focus of the other sex's sexual desire. We're talking about different body shapes, hair distribution (for want of a better phrase!) and genitals. And there are, of course, the internal differences too—different bodily organs and some differences of size in certain structures of male and female brains.

Inevitably, this leads to very different thinking and behavior. In conflict with the feminist agenda of the 1970s and 1980s, the 1990s bestseller *Men Are from Mars, Women Are from Venus* made its author rich through pointing out how radically different male and female attitudes and actions can be after all. But we don't have to trust a controversial pop psychologist on this; throughout human history, so many other books (for example, *Pride and Prejudice*), plays (such as *Much Ado About Nothing*) and TV series (such as *Friends*) have made similar points—as if daily interactions between the sexes weren't evidence enough.

So there are undeniable physical and psychological differences between men and women. We aren't exactly the same. While we are right to insist on the equality of all men and women, we have got it wrong when we maintain that we are all exactly the same and thus interchangeable.

But where does this leave us? Saying that men and women are "equal but different"? Now that slogan has unfortunate echoes of apartheid South Africa. Yet it is essentially what God's Word teaches—and what human life shows. Perhaps we could say that we enjoy "a different state but the same status," but that sounds like a phrase borrowed from devolutionary politics. So let's stick with "equal but different" until someone comes up with a better summary of what the Bible teaches. If you have one, I'd really like to know.

Exploring the Difference

But *why* the difference? This question merits more attention than coming up with a better slogan. With all the pressure to see women and men as exactly the same (despite all the evidence to the contrary), it would help our case to know exactly why we want to fight to preserve the obvious distinction between the sexes and oppose their interchangeability.

And the problem here is that many of the church's traditional answers to these questions are pastorally disastrous and, more importantly, unconvincing biblically. Most contain an element of truth but have been asked to carry more freight than they can bear.

So throughout church history, the majority have said the reason for sexual difference is procreation. That God primarily created the two sexes so that there could be children. Now, science has never been an area of strength for me, but there would seem to a strong biological case for this—as well as a strong theological one. Genesis 1:27 (the creation of the two sexes) is immediately followed by God ordering those sexes to go and have sex so that there will be more of them. Sexual difference is essential to humankind's survival and flourishing.

But to say that this is the primary reason for sexual difference is theologically problematic. There is, for instance, the New Testament's emphasis on the importance of your spiritual descendants rather than your biological family tree. This is a comfort in a world where many are infertile or never get to have children for other reasons. Pastorally, it is obviously helpful to be able to say to a single woman, or an infertile man, that they have not missed out on the only thing they were created as a woman or man to do.

So is the primary reason instead companionship? This has become an increasingly popular explanation, with apparent biblical warrant in a verse like Genesis 2:18. Here God seems to create Eve for Adam just to solve the problem of the first man's loneliness. Her appearance and their marriage complete him—all his needs are met as he meets his "other half." Sexual difference allows two human beings to come together and complete each other.

But this is again problematic in a world in which many struggle to find their other half and experience this feeling of completion. Many have apparently found their other half and still don't share that experience! Sexual difference obviously created the possibility of companionship for the first man—with both Eve and the children that they brought into this world—but because of that first sexual union, other kinds of companionship are now open to humanity in lots of different contexts. Companionship is possible without finding one person of the opposite sex to complete us.

Another primary reason for sexual difference, according to others, is the difference in the God-given roles that women and men have. Personally, I believe that God has given the sexes different roles in both church and biological families, but I still don't think this is the main driving force behind sexual difference, and I wouldn't want to build such an important truth on such controversial foundations.

So we're still left asking: Why the difference? What is the primary reason we've all been created either male or female?

Grasping God's Love

The Bible's overwhelmingly convincing answer is this: to help us grasp the passionate nature of God's love for his people. Catholic teacher Christopher West writes this:

> God made us as sexual beings—as men and women with a desire for union—precisely to tell the story of his love for us. In the biblical view, the fulfillment of love between the sexes is a great foreshadowing of something quite literally "out of this world"—the infinite bliss and ecstasy that awaits us in heaven.[3]

God created the two sexes—and sex—in this world as a trailer for life in the world to come. To help us understand the power of his love for us in the here and now, and the pleasure that will be ours when we live with him in his new heaven and earth. As film directors put romantic scenes in their trailers to make us want to go to their movies, God has put sex on this planet to make us want to go to heaven.

Really? Consider for a moment the prominence of marriage and sex throughout the Bible—and how often they are used as a picture of God's love for his people. The bookends of the Bible help establish this point: the whole thing starts with the marriage of a man and a woman and its consummation (Genesis 1–2), and its great narrative ends with the marriage of a groom to his bride and its consummation (Revelation 21–22). The very first human marriage (and all those that follow) are there to point us to how things will end: with the eternal marriage of the divine bridegroom (God in Christ) to his chosen human bride (God's people). All of human history is just the journey up the aisle.

Does this all seem a bit far-fetched? Then just remember how often the Bible uses the picture of marriage of a man and a woman to talk of the reality of God's love for his people. Go read Ezekiel 16 and Hosea 1–3 to see God provocatively using human experience of heterosexual marriage and sex to help his people grasp the horror of their unfaithfulness to him in the light of his constant love for them. The spiritual adultery of God's people is the most powerful illustration God's prophets ever use to help them grasp their sin and the pain it brings their jilted God.

In the Old Testament, we also find the Song of Songs, which, for most of church history, has been correctly understood as a love duet between God and his people. More recently, it's tended to be applied to love and romance between the sexes, which is a valid application, but it is primarily about God's love for us. We shouldn't be embarrassed by the sexual passion that it seems to involve (on both sides) and presume it must be more about human love as a result. Throughout the Old Testament, God seems to have no hesitation in describing his love for his people in sexual terms. In fact, he seems deliberately to take and use sexual language that he knows will most effectively communicate to us sexual beings the full power of his love for us.

All of this paves the way (as the Old Testament always does) for Jesus and for John the Baptist's description of him as the bridegroom of God's people (John 3:28-29), and Jesus' own use of this language to describe himself (Matthew 9:15). This idea is then famously developed by Paul in Ephesians 5 as he shows how the marital relationship between a husband and wife is patterned on Christ's similar relationship with his church. So intertwined are the two relationships in his theology that Paul quotes Genesis 2:24 and sees it as applying not only to human marriage (as we would expect) but also to the marriage of God's Son to God's people.

All of this biblical theology is then, of course, wonderfully brought together in the book of Revelation where the Lamb (Jesus) is getting married to his bride (God's people throughout history) in chapters 19, 21 and 22. It's presented as the consummation of all God's loving plans and purposes for his people: *the* great wedding that all the others have been preparing us for.

Eminent New Testament scholar N. T. Wright recently reflected on the significance of all of this:

> The last scene in the Bible is the new heaven and the new earth, and the symbol for that is the marriage of Christ and his church. It's not just one or two verses here and there which say this or that. It's an entire narrative which works with this complementarity so that a male-plus-female marriage is a signpost or a signal about the goodness of the original creation and God's intention for the eventual new heavens and new earth.[4]

Do you get the point that he draws from all of this biblical imagery? Marriage between a man and a woman—that complementary union of sexual difference—is central to the very wiring of God's plan for the universe, from its beginning and into eternity. So, change its constituent parts (a man and a woman), and you are interfering with where God has said his world is heading—to the unity in difference of the heavenly marriage of the divine and human.

This is why marriage has often been defined as a sacrament, as (like baptism and the Lord's Supper) an earthly representation of a spiritual reality. It is a divinely drawn picture that points us to a greater reality, and its constituent points are not interchangeable as a result. People would, rightly, not consider changing the water in baptism (with all it symbolizes) for another liquid. The Lord's Supper would not correctly represent all that it is meant to if the wine were traded for Coke and the bread for some curly fries. So we can't make marriage anything but the permanent sexual union of a man and a woman without undermining its central purpose of pointing us to the passionate consummation of God's love for his people.

Knowing all of this is why my favorite moment of any wedding is when the groom looks down the aisle to see his bride walking toward him. That moment reminds me of Jesus looking down the aisle of history to his church with the same look of love on his face. That look being exchanged between two men or two women would imply that Jesus' role could be taken by any of us—that there is no essential difference between God and his people. That is not the case—and so that is not possible. Sexual difference matters that much.

C. S. Lewis is, as ever, helpful on this, although speaking into a different argument (the ordination of women as Anglican priests):

The kind of equality which implies that the equals are interchangeable (like counters or identical machines) is, among humans, a legal fiction. It may be a useful fiction, but in church we turn our back on fictions. One of the ends for which sex was created was to symbolize to us the hidden things of God. One of the functions of human marriage is to express the nature of the union between Christ and the Church. We have no authority to take the living and seminal figures which God has painted on the canvas of our nature and shift them about as if they were mere geometrical figures.[5]

His words speak with greater potency and relevance into the argument over same-sex marriage. Men and women are equal (we can never repeat that fact enough), but they are not exactly the same and not interchangeable—they are different, and that is theologically so significant. Our view on the morality of same-sex unions needs to rest on this sort of solid biblical anthropology.

Living with Difference

But, of course, all of this is very painful for me and the thousands of other Christian men and women like me who would love to marry someone of their own sex, who wish we could change the essence of marriage. How do we cope with this clear message of the importance of sexual difference when we desire to have sex with someone of our own gender? Surely, for people like me, this is a message that leads to nothing but a negative view of sexual difference and our sexuality. Not necessarily! I think Catholic scholar Christopher Roberts helps us:

Sexual difference . . . is the only distinction that implicates everyone. Humans can resent this distinction, and our life in this sphere can be marred by sin and imperfection, but, in the end, our own humanity depends upon finding ways of life that are premised on gratitude for it. To be what we are, we find ways of life that thank God for having made us male and female. To be fully human and follow Christ faithfully, there are many things we must do, but among them must be some sort of embrace of sexual difference.[6]

I somehow need to embrace what the Bible teaches about the importance of sexual difference, despite the restrictions it puts on my preferred expression of it. To view sexuality as a good thing, even though God bans me from acting out my desires in a sexual relationship with another man. How can I do that? By believing that, like all that God says to me, it is actually good for me (remember Psalm 19?).

A couple of ways (there are many more) of grasping this goodness, and of thinking positively about my sexuality, have recently been suggested to me.

One is just a simple recognition that sexual difference makes heterosexual married relationships harder but better. Melinda Selmys is a same-sex attracted Christian who has been in sexual relationships with both a woman (in the past) and a man (she's now married with children). She perceptively writes:

It is because of, and not in spite of, the tensions between the sexes that marriage works. Masculinity and femininity each have their vices and their strengths. The difficulty when you have two women or two men together is that they understand each other too well, and are thus inclined more to excuse than forgive. That frank bafflement which inevitably sets in, in any heterosexual relationship ("Why on earth would he do that? I just don't understand . . .")

never set in throughout all of the years that my girlfriend and I were together—naturally enough. We were both women, and we chose each other because we seemed to be particularly compatible women.[7]

Not being of a different gender from your marriage partner takes away some of the healthy tension that makes a good marriage. Your gendered similarities (despite the other human differences) undermine the unity in difference that marriage is supposed to be all about. It is not as good as the real thing, and God wants his people to have what is best for them—thus his ban on it.

But then surely my sexuality can be nothing more than a negative aspect of my life—if there is no prospect of me changing enough to be able to consummate a heterosexual marriage. Not if I pay attention to these precious words of pastor John Piper:

> The *ultimate* reason (not the only one) why we are sexual is to make God more deeply knowable. The language and imagery of sexuality are the most graphic and most powerful that the Bible uses to describe the relationship between God and his people—both positively (when we are faithful) and negatively (when we are not).[8]

I've most grasped God's love for me when I've seen it in terms of a man's love for his wife, when I've read passages like Ezekiel 16 and felt the full passion of his love for me. My sexuality has allowed me to understand and appreciate the incredible power of the sexual language that God uses there and elsewhere: to communicate the passionate nature of his love for people like *me*! My sexuality might not lead me into a loving marriage, but it does consistently lead me into a greater appreciation of God's love for me in Christ. That is one of many reasons why I'm profoundly grateful for it.

Explaining the Difference

All of this leaves the church today with a massive challenge: to articulate the equality of the two sexes at the same time as the differences and then to explain the importance of these differences and why we need to preserve them. This is a challenge we must meet if we truly want what God says about sexuality to sound both good and plausible today. The lead needs to be taken by our churches' pastors, but they will probably only have the courage if you encourage them. So ask your pastor(s) for some teaching and discussion on all of this as soon as they can provide the best context for it. We will all benefit from it. In the meantime, why not pick up your Bible, turn to one of the passages that talks about God's marriage (in Christ) to the church and bask in the passionate intensity of his love for us? We are the object of the greatest love story ever told. And, this time, it's actually true. And it will last forever.

Application Question

How can we better explain the need for sexual difference in the union of marriage?

"Godliness is heterosexuality."

I was recently on a panel talking about same-sex attraction at a large Christian conference. One of the questions I was asked was a thinly veiled version of the one question that many Christian parents most want to ask me: "How can I stop my children from being same-sex attracted?" or (as no one has really had the courage to put it), "How I can I stop my child from becoming like you?"

It's a revealing question. The number of times I've been asked it (always in roundabout ways) demonstrates how great a fear it is for many Christian parents—to raise a child that might be sexually attracted to their own sex. It's not something that they want to have to share in the Christmas letter in years to come—either openly or by what's clearly left unsaid. The great hope is that they will be able to write of happy marriages, numerous grandchildren and continued involvement in a good evangelical church. They don't want to have to say instead that a child is gay, that there won't be any grandchildren (at least, not in the conventional way) and that their son or daughter is now part of some LGBT-affirming church (if any church at all). What they want from me is a few simple steps they can take to stop that from happening—ban their young son from playing with his sister's doll's house and discourage that sister from playing football when she's older.

Why the paranoia (a word honestly used by a Christian parent asking me this question)? It's because, in the evangelical church, godliness is heterosexuality and no one can really grasp how same-sex attraction and godliness could ever exist together. So if you want your child to be godly, you must do all you can now to ensure that they are heterosexual. And, obviously, if your child starts experiencing same-sex attraction, you must then do all you can to change that as quickly as you can.

All of this explains how much time, effort and money some evangelical churches have invested in counseling that promises a permanent change in someone's sexuality. Many same-sex attracted children of evangelical parents have been signed up for reparative therapy or sent off on residential courses that will "heal" them of their same-sex attraction. Often the children (and sometimes the parents) have then given up on evangelical Christianity when these attempts have failed. If godliness is heterosexuality, what's the point of trying to be a Christian when you're not heterosexual?

It's tragic that this link has been made in people's minds. But I understand why: it is a link that has often been at the forefront of my mind too. If heterosexuality is godliness, the big change that's most been needed in my life is for me to become heterosexual. And so I've prayed hard and searched hard for an effective antidote to my same-sex attraction. The pursuit of holiness has nearly always equaled the pursuit of heterosexuality for me.

So I was helped enormously—hopefully like everybody else listening—by the reply of another panel member at that conference to this question. A heterosexual church minister, he runs his church's support group for same-sex attracted church family members. He's also the married father of two sons. He said something like this: "We, most of all, want our boys to grow up as godly and mature Christians. Some of the most godly and mature Christians we know are same-sex attracted. So why should we be so afraid of them growing up as same-sex attracted?"

I was (and I think this is the correct use of the word) flabbergasted by this reply. It finally blew apart my wrong presumption that same-sex attraction and godliness, like oil and water, don't ever mix. It made me recall that some of the most godly people that I have ever known are those who've also experienced same-sex attraction. In fact, one of the Christian leaders I most respect as godly has been made so *through* his struggle with same-sex attraction. I'd just never heard the link made so obviously and in such a moving way and context.

Godliness Promotion

But that panel member is a parent whose main ambition for his children is the right one—godliness, not heterosexuality. I'm sure it doesn't mean that he's praying that his boys will grow up to be same-sex attracted; he'll understandably want them to avoid my kitchen floor moments. But his reply showed that he has what we should all really care about in our response to the gospel of grace—Christ-likeness. Being like Jesus is the true biblical definition of godliness.

Paul's clear passion for the Ephesian church is that they will reflect who they now are in Jesus. He says to Christians like us: because of all that you now are in Jesus (chaps. 1–3), you are to be like Jesus (chaps. 4–6). Just one example comes from the start of chapter 5: "Follow God's example, therefore, as dearly loved children and walk in the way of love, just as Christ loved us and gave himself up for us as a fragrant offering and sacrifice to God" (Ephesians 5:1-2). As God's children (that's our new status in Jesus), we are to imitate him, to love like him—in the same sort of way that led Jesus to sacrifice himself in our place on the cross. That's the sort of love he personified and demonstrated for us in human history.

And, interestingly, it is sexual ethics that Paul applies all this to next. True Christlike, self-sacrificial love means saying no to any sexual activity outside marriage (Ephesians 5:3), as well as giving up a whole host of other attitudes and actions. But, crucially, this call to sexual purity is a subsection of godliness, not *the* definition of it.

I need to hear this. My guess is that you do too. When we are at our best, we do get this. But so often we show that we have forgotten it. As a result, we probably all need to be corrected by the perceptive observation of anthropologist Jenell Williams Paris. She writes, "The 'end' of a holy life is to be like Christ. When it comes to sexual holiness, however, the end is often misperceived as a life station (heterosexual marriage) instead of a quality of life (Christ-likeness)."[1] Those words are so helpful to me. God most wants me to grow more like Jesus, not to be married to a woman. So my failure to achieve the latter does not mean I'm making no progress on the former.

What has so often encouraged me to give up on the Christian life has been my lack of progress in becoming heterosexual. I've never been sexually attracted to a woman. Yet every so often, a short period of not being sexually attracted to a man has given me hope—only for it to be dashed when my type of good-looking man has walked onto my TV screen or into my life.

As a result, I've kept feeling I'm making no progress as a Christian—still struggling with the same wrong sexual desires I did back when I was sixteen. That's when it has felt least plausible to keep going as a Christian. Feeling like you have made no steps forward for twenty years makes you unwilling to keep going.

So this attitude that godliness is heterosexuality is a very dangerous one. It is spiritually life-threatening for people like me. We need to discourage it whenever we meet it. Instead, in line with our Bibles, we need to measure Christian maturity by Christlikeness. Of course, that will involve monitoring sexual purity, but we also need to examine our greed, our everyday conversation, *all* the patterns of idolatry that there are in our lives.

I've certainly found it much more spiritually healthy not to be totally preoccupied by my sexuality and its failure to change. Remembering the call to be like Jesus in everything has shown me not only the countless other ways I'm *not* like Jesus but also the progress I have actually been making in becoming more like him over the last twenty years. This progress has often come in the midst of, and as a direct result of, my enduring struggle with same-sex attraction.

A Catalyst for Real Godliness

Let me give you an example: I do self-righteousness well. I'm your classic well-behaved firstborn son, who keeps the rules and is scandalized when others don't. Pity my naughty little sister who had to grow up with my censoriousness, which was already perfected by age six. It was toxic for my relationship with her back then, and the poison has kept spreading ever since. It's led to both a judgmental attitude to anyone who breaks the rules I keep and a sense of entitlement that often makes me feel God has wrongly denied me the things I've earned. I'm the older brother in Jesus' parable (Luke 15:11-32). It's scary.

It would probably be self-righteous to say that my self-righteousness is gone today. But it has been an area of godliness that I've been making progress in. How has God achieved that? Well, he's used an interesting mix. He's given me his Word to demand change in this area (1 Corinthians 13:4). He's given me his Spirit to empower that change (Galatians 5:16). He's given me the motivation to change in the gospel (Titus 2:11-14). *And* he's used my struggle with same-sex attraction to force the change. It's hard to be self-righteous about other people's sexual sins when your status as a sexual sinner is made very clear to you by God. It's hard to preserve your sense of entitlement when you know those sins demand a death sentence but instead you get eternal life for free at God's expense. My same-sex attraction has directly led to godliness: they *can* exist together. I would be less godly in this area of my life without it.

Nothing has given me more childlike dependence on God than my same-sex attraction—and, after all, that's what being a Christian is about, according to Jesus (Mark 10:15). I so often don't know how I'm going to stay sexually pure—I am so acutely aware of the weaknesses that could lead me into scandalous sin tomorrow that I'm forced to depend on God in prayer. It's my same-sex attraction that has again and again made me recognize the fiction that I can live an independent life without God's help. Same-sex attraction and godliness *do* mix: in fact, the spiritual chemical reaction they produce (if I can call it that) is very powerful indeed.

One last example: there has also been a growing sense that what I thought was the large iceberg that would sink me (my sexuality) is just the tip of the even larger iceberg of perfectionism that is much more of a spiritual danger in every part of my life. Just focusing in on the tip has been one of the devil's most successful strategies in blinding me to the full danger I am in because of the deeper idolatry in my life (of which my sexuality is just a symptom). Like many others, I've been helped by

Tim Keller's distinction between the surface idols in our lives (for me, a certain type of perfect beauty in a man) and the deeper idols that drive them (for me, an unhealthy insistence on perfection in every area of life).[2] It's on the deeper idols like this that I need to focus my efforts for change and greater Christlikeness. My same-sex attraction has been the most visible sign of much deeper problems that I would never have confronted without it.

Am I saying that my same-sex attraction has done nothing but good in my life, that my sexuality isn't marred by sin? No. Various examples I've given in the pages of this book have shown that not to be true. It has been the cause of a huge amount of ungodliness in my life. But it has been the means of huge growth in godliness too.

Am I saying that no one who experiences same-sex attraction should seek to change their sexual desires? No. We should want ungodliness to go. We know that with God, all things are possible. Yet we also need to remember that he doesn't promise the restoration of all things in this world—but in the world to come. We wouldn't guarantee a paralyzed man complete physical healing in the here and now. I don't think we can guarantee a same-sex attracted man complete sexual healing in the here and now either.

I have heard enough convincing stories to know that changes in sexuality can happen (to some extent) for some, while remaining seemingly impossible for others.[3] So I want to urge all same-sex attracted Christians (and their church families) not to see progress in Christlikeness purely in terms of steps forward or backward in reshaping their sexual orientation. To stake everything on one area of thought and behavior is not a biblical approach to godliness. It is often a disastrous thing to do if those people want to stay trusting in Jesus—especially if he doesn't one day give them a partner of the opposite sex and kids.

What needs to be heard more is what the Bible says: that the gospel of grace demands Christlikeness of us in *every* area of life. That's what our children need to hear from us so that if they grow up to be same-sex attracted, they don't conclude that they can't be Christians, but instead see this as just another challenging context (among many others) in which to become more and more like Jesus, all in response to the most challenging context of all—the cross—that he went through for us.

An End to Sexual Hypocrisy

What we also need is, of course, a constant recognition that a heterosexual sexuality does not guarantee godliness in this area of life. This might sound obvious, but we have to recognize that homosexual sex outside marriage is perceived as a much greater sin in our churches than heterosexual sex outside marriage. Why? The Bible would condemn both in similar terms (Leviticus 20:10, 12). The same sin has been committed. The same must be true of sexual fantasy—whether its focus is on someone of the same sex or opposite sex; both would surely qualify as adultery in Jesus' eyes (Matthew 5:27-28). Yet, for some reason, I always feel that my homosexual fantasies must be worse. If same-sex attracted Christians feel they are being held to a higher standard than anyone else in the church, the plausibility problem will only get worse. Christian psychologist Mark Yarhouse raises this issue:

> My experience is that those who struggle with homosexuality are quite aware of and sensitive to hypocrisy in the church. They know when they are being asked to do something that others are not. If you agree that sexual minorities could benefit from following a curriculum of Christlikeness, then follow that curriculum in your own life. It is always

better to lead by example, which will give you credibility to speak to the benefits of following such a curriculum. Put differently, if you believe in stewarding your sexuality, then lead by example, living out the principles you promote.[4]

So do you want to make sexual godliness seem plausible to people like me? Take Christlikeness seriously in every area of your life. But do also be sexually godly yourself. Don't demand anything of me that you are unwilling to demand of yourself. And when I have to confess my sexual sins to you, don't be afraid to confess your sexual sins to me. In that way, we can spur each other on to Christlikeness and on to love and good deeds through the triumphs and tragedies.

Greater honesty about the challenges of being sexual beings has been one of the upsides of the so-called sexual revolution. Unlike many of the downsides, this honesty has yet to spread to the church. Some of us same-sex attracted pastors have recently taken a lead, but we have yet to be followed by the brothers and sisters in Christ who struggle with internet porn, who have survived the pain of adultery or who live in sexless marriages. Now, honesty is not always the best policy in such deeply personal matters, but until some go public with their private struggles (or, at least, until we start to recognize publicly that they are issues with which many church members are grappling), the church will continue to be perceived as sexually self-righteous—rather than a place where all who are sexually broken (which is all of us!) can get the help and support we need. Many will have to struggle on alone in silence.

What can you do to help change this? Well, do your Christian friends (including your same-sex attracted ones) know that you struggle to express your sexuality in godly ways too? You might not share all the details, but it will help them to know that you struggle alongside them. Such confession might lead to a massive step forward in godliness for us all, as pastor Dietrich Bonhoeffer explains:

> In confession the break-through to community takes place. Sin demands to have a man by himself. It withdraws him from the community. The more isolated a person is, the more destructive will be the power of sin over him, and the more deeply he becomes involved in it, the more disastrous is his isolation. Sin wants to remain unknown. It shuns the light. In the darkness of the unexpressed it poisons the whole being of a person.[5]

One of the best things we could all do to break the power of sexual sin in all of our lives in all of our churches is confess, in appropriate contexts and ways, our sexual sins to one another. Could you be part of making that happen?

Application Question

How can we all make sure that we aren't appearing to be sexually self-righteousness?

MISSTEP #8

"Celibacy is bad for you."

In his excellent book on marriage, Christopher Ash poses this question: "When did we last see a successful movie which portrayed a contented bachelor or spinster?"[1]

I never have. Have you?[2] The basic premise of Hollywood comedies like *The 40-Year-Old Virgin* and *40 Days and 40 Nights* demonstrates this—the first chronicles a man's increasingly desperate attempts to have sex for the first time; in the second another younger man struggles to last just forty days and nights without it. In the world around us, celibacy is a bad thing, to be avoided at almost any cost.

And that's true inside the church too. When did we last hear a good sermon that promoted lifelong singleness? I never have. Have you? When tackled, singleness is usually spoken of as a temporary problem happily solved by marriage. You're taught how to survive until your wedding day—not how to thrive as a single woman or man until your dying day. Again, celibacy is a bad thing to be avoided at almost any cost.

There have been times in church history when the opposite has been true—when marriage has been portrayed as bad and celibacy as good. But at present, we seem to be rather stuck at the opposite end of the spectrum. There are even some parts of the church where singleness past around twenty-five years of age is seen as a bit of a problem. I once had a conversation with a Christian leader in which the opening questions were about my age (then twenty-six) and marital status (single), and the third question was "Why aren't you married?" Not to be paired up by then was a real problem in his mind. A single friend in his early thirties felt (and was treated) like a museum piece in this church context. For some reason, the evangelical church doesn't like celibacy today.

It is, of course, easy to understand why. If you're a church leader who, rightly, wants his church family to keep sex within marriage, you can see how encouraging people to get married as soon as possible seems the most plausible way of ensuring that in today's sex-obsessed society. I suspect that recent sex scandals within the Roman Catholic priesthood have also increased the perceived dangers of not having sex at all: if not allowed to express itself rightly, will a repressed sexuality inevitably express itself wrongly?

But, as I hope I've demonstrated back in misstep number five, no sex does not necessarily mean a lack of healthy intimacy or the unhealthy repression of a person's sexuality. And, as we discovered in the same chapter, it does not need to mean the loneliness that many fear either. Church family is God's answer to his own observation that it is not good for a human being to be alone (Genesis 2:18). Pastorally, I've actually discovered more loneliness in marriages than among single people because marriage can isolate people from their friends; it's always worse in a context where no one expects it.

And yet the evangelical church still manages to communicate that celibacy is a bad thing. Despite honoring the worldwide impact of the ministry of a single man like the late John Stott, we still manage to discourage people from copying him. People are incomplete until they've met their "other half"—although talk of a man and a woman becoming "one flesh" in marriage (Genesis 2:24) is stressing their permanent (and sexual) union rather than saying they are incomplete beforehand.

The results in my life were long-term campaigns by well-intentioned friends to marry me off. They used wedding seating plans, paired me off with suitable women to run things at church, made subtle (and unsubtle) suggestions and berated me for my lack of cooperation with their carefully laid plans. All of this was at best embarrassing, and sometimes painful, for me *and* the other victims of their schemes.

Those friends obviously meant no harm. And I became good at appreciating the love and concern for me that their efforts always showed. But I wasn't being encouraged to think that the celibacy I had committed myself to was worth living. Life is much easier now that I've been more open.

And if we don't communicate that celibacy is a plausible way of living, we make it almost inevitable for same-sex attracted Christians (and those who care for them) to embrace gay "marriage." If the alternative is a life of dangerous repression and acute loneliness, no wonder people are deserting the traditional definition of marriage in droves. Until we rehabilitate celibacy as a good thing, they will continue to do so.

Rehabilitating Celibacy

And celibacy *is* a good thing. Our Bibles make that very clear. The good sermon we've never heard that promotes lifelong singleness is there in 1 Corinthians 7. Paul is the preacher, and he manages to promote both the gifts of marriage and singleness at the same time, in a way that most generations have failed to do. But it is, of course, his teaching on singleness that is most striking and challenging to us today. As a single man himself, he commends it as a way of life: "I wish that all of you were as I am. But each of you has your own gift from God; one has this gift, another has that" (1 Corinthians 7:7).

Why does he say what I've never heard a church leader say today? How can he be so enthusiastic about celibacy? Call it a gift, a gift that you automatically have unless it has been replaced by the gift of marriage?[3] Does he not understand the human sex drive? Yes! He spends much of this chapter showing that he understands it only too well. Was he not aware of the problem of loneliness? Yes! He just lived his life in community in another way. Instead, for him, being a single man actually made life easier, not harder. That's why he was so enthusiastic about it! That's why he promotes it here. Later on, he makes this pragmatic point:

> I would like you to be free from concern. An unmarried man is concerned about the Lord's affairs—how he can please the Lord. But a married man is concerned about the affairs of this world—how he can please his wife—and his interests are divided. An unmarried woman or virgin is concerned about the Lord's affairs: Her aim is to be devoted to the Lord in both body and spirit. But a married woman is concerned about the affairs of this world—how she can please her husband. I am saying this for your own good, not to restrict you, but that you may live in a right way in undivided devotion to the Lord. (1 Corinthians 7:32-35)

Paul says that being single makes the Christian life easier. Following Jesus is all about pleasing our new Lord and Savior Jesus.

That is much easier to do if you can focus your attention on doing that entirely—if you don't also have to try to please a husband or wife, as you should if you are married.

The obvious truth of this has been proved to me time and time again. It's shown in how comparatively easy it is for me to listen and talk to God as I read my Bible and pray: my married friends have to negotiate this time with at least one other person— sometimes with a whole family's complicated daily routine. I am also able to give much more time, energy and money than they are to the Christian ministry to which God has called me: they have to balance numerous other calls against these precious things. Paul has it right: it *is* much easier for me to be whole-hearted in my devotion to Jesus (although I still don't find it easy, despite these advantages).

And the obvious result is that it is going to be much easier for me to achieve more for Jesus too. Church history teaches this. Many of the most significant and inspiring steps forward in world evangelization were made by single Christians (or married ones who wrongly behaved as if they were single, such as William Carey). David Brainerd's ministry to Native Americans would be one famous example; Gladys Aylward's work in China would be another. They only achieved what they did for Jesus because they were single and could be fully devoted to their ministry for him.

This clear benefit of being single was a reality that the early church clearly recognized. But it's important for us to see it as both practically *and* theologically significant. Professor Stanley Hauerwas makes this point:

> Singleness was legitimate, not because sex was thought to be a particularly questionable activity, but because the mission of the church was such that "between the times"

the church required those who were very capable of complete service to the kingdom. And we must remember that the "sacrifice" made by the single is not that of "giving up sex," but the much more significant sacrifice of giving up heirs. There can be no more radical act than this, as it is the clearest institutional expression that one's future is not guaranteed by the family, but by the church. The church, the harbinger of the kingdom of God, is now the source of our primary loyalty.[4]

Paul and those like him gave up, more significantly to them, children—not just sex. That is still a big thing in today's society and was a massive thing back then. Not to have an heir in a patriarchal society was a huge sacrifice—no one would continue your name. Why did they make this sacrifice? For people like you and me! So that the early church they served would have spiritual descendants and so that the good news of the gospel would go further than Palestine and just one or two Jewish generations. And the worldwide church of today is what Paul and his single-minded followers down the ages have, through God's grace, achieved. We should be more positive about singleness as a result. Celibacy is a good thing. We wouldn't be Christians today without it.

Many of us have also benefited from contemporary examples of the gospel power of celibacy: the single woman who devotedly ran the Sunday school through which we first met Jesus, the books of that bachelor who could write so much because he had no wife or kids, the prayers of that maiden aunt who was, as a result of her singleness, able to devote so much time to praying for your conversion and those of many others.

Personally, I owe much to two single men who, because of their celibacy, were able to devote a huge amount of time to me at significant stages of my Christian life; both have gone on to serve the church in Africa in trying circumstances that would have been difficult to expose any family to.

And even if you can't think of similar examples in your own life, all Christians are indebted to someone else who stayed single for the gospel: Jesus himself. Living in the same patriarchal society as Paul, he remained celibate, and we wrongly downplay his humanity if we don't think that he would have been tempted to settle down with a wife, sex and kids. Why didn't he? He remained single for us—those things were not compatible with God's salvation plan for him to live, die and rise again in our place.

And some of what motivated him in doing all of that should motivate people today to embrace the single life too. Remember some of the opening words of Hebrews 12:

> [Let us fix] our eyes on Jesus, the pioneer and perfecter of faith. For the joy set before him he endured the cross, scorning its shame, and sat down at the right hand of the throne of God. (Hebrews 12:2)

Jesus gave up everything for us partly because of the reward he knew would be his as a result—the "joy set before him." He went through the greatest of pains, knowing that one day soon it would be worth it. And having stressed the gospel potential of celibacy, I don't want to underplay the great pain it can often bring. But I do want to say that it will be worth it for us too. For Jesus is wonderfully going to share that joy with his brothers and sisters for all of eternity.

I've been really helped in my own commitment to lifelong celibacy by this eternal perspective stressed by Catholic teacher Christopher West:

Celibacy for the kingdom is not a declaration that sex is "bad." It's a declaration that while sex can be awesome, there's something even better—*infinitely better!* Christian celibacy is a bold declaration that heaven is *real*, and it is worth selling everything to possess.[5]

I know there are many today who think that it is a great tragedy to die a virgin. But I hope I will. Because I know that I will not have lost out on anything too significant. Because the Bible teaches me that I will have missed only the brief foretaste that sex is meant to be of the eternal reality of the perfect union between Christ and his church that I will one day experience forever (Revelation 21:1-5). Any fleeting pleasure I've given up in the meantime will be more than worth it then.

So celibacy *is* a plausible way to live. We need to repent of hiding that fact. And we need more and more lives that demonstrate it plausibly today—not only for the benefit of same-sex attracted Christians like me but also for the benefit of the whole church.

How, then, does your church celebrate God's gift of celibacy? My guess is that you'll have a good track record when it comes to promoting marriage (weddings celebrated, numerous sermons on the subject, a course and books recommended from the front) but not much success when it comes to commending singleness. How could you celebrate the single members of your church family? I can think of an example from one church I was part of: we used a single woman's eightieth birthday as a chance to thank her (and her Father God) for all she had given us using her gift of celibacy to build up our church family. I suspect we could have done more to encourage her over the decades, but it was, I hope, better late than never. You can often tell what an organization values by what (or whom) they celebrate—we need to be better at celebrating all of the Christlike single men and women (for whatever reason) in our midst. They have been given a precious gift that deserves a party or two as much as any marriage does.

Application Question

How can we all be as affirming of singleness as the Bible is?

MISSTEP #9

"Suffering is to be avoided."

The intention of this book has been to make my life seem plausible (to both you and me). But I'm conscious of how I've undermined that aim every time I've described how hard it is, how much suffering it brings. I wish I could just have made it sound all nice and easy and enjoyable. But it isn't. So I haven't.

And that is a big plausibility problem in today's world— perhaps the greatest. For these days, all too often, we see suffering as something to be avoided. As we established earlier, we pursue happiness. If something makes you really suffer, you stop doing it. If something will make you happy, you sign up for it. So why on earth would anyone sign up for a life of suffering as a celibate same-sex attracted Christian? And how can I encourage others to do the same?

In a word: Jesus. For he teaches us that suffering for a good purpose is not to be avoided but embraced. Once his disciples had understood who he was (God's long-promised Messiah), this was the first thing that Jesus (the Son of Man) told them:

He then began to teach them that the Son of Man must suffer many things and be rejected by the elders, the chief priests and the teachers of the law, and that he must be killed and after three days rise again. (Mark 8:31)

Jesus came to suffer: he exchanged the comfort of heaven for an earthly life of suffering and a death that was the greatest act of human suffering *ever*. Suffering is what his life on this planet was all about.

That reality was obviously not comfortable for him—and it is an uncomfortable truth for his followers too. What happens next illustrates this:

> He spoke plainly about this, and Peter took him aside and began to rebuke him.
>
> But when Jesus turned and looked at his disciples, he rebuked Peter. "Get behind me, Satan!" he said. "You do not have in mind the concerns of God, but merely human concerns." (Mark 8:32-33)

Suffering was as unpopular then as it is now. It's not what Peter was looking for in a leader and it's not what we look for either. We prefer the idea of a successful king to a suffering one. Why? Because we see the implications: follow a successful king and you share in his success; follow a suffering king and you share in his sufferings. Jesus makes this crystal clear: "Then he called the crowd to him along with his disciples and said: 'Whoever wants to be my disciple must deny themselves and take up their cross and follow me'" (Mark 8:34). Jesus calls us to suffer too. Following a suffering Messiah makes suffering inevitable. He went to the cross—his disciples will have to go the way of the cross too.

And the disciples who first heard these words soon discovered the truth of them. They watched Jesus suffer and die (and rise again), and then they suffered and died for him, some on crosses as he did. Generations of other Christians have done the same: suffered by sacrificing their lives like Jesus. That's how these words have reached people like you and me.

But, for some reason, in our generation, following Jesus is no longer about our sacrifice and suffering. Western Christians have, by and large, stopped denying ourselves—we now talk more about our right to be ourselves. Our Christian lives are more about self-gratification—seemingly denying the existence of Jesus' words here. They are a continuation of our previous lives, with a thin Christian veneer: just being nicer to a few more people.

The crosses we bear are the small annoyances we haven't yet managed to rid ourselves of (a bad knee, our interfering mother-in-law, a bad boss at work), rather than any significant suffering we intentionally embrace because we are following Jesus and want others to follow him too. We've chosen to ignore the fact that Jesus is here calling his disciples to make a conscious and costly decision to sacrifice ourselves, to say no to things we might want, even deserve or need, because that's what it means to follow his example.

WWJD were the letters on the ubiquitous bracelets and other paraphernalia some years back: What would Jesus do? One problem with asking that question in our generation was how few people had asked another question: What *did* Jesus do? WDJD would have been a much more useful question to ask because it would have encouraged us all to reflect on the motivation and model that his life of self-sacrificial suffering on this earth provides. We would have remembered that he came to suffer and calls us to suffer too. We would have been encouraged rightly to deny ourselves for him because of all that he denied himself so that we could be right with God.

Our contemporary Christian lives of comfort are not the Jesus way. He couldn't make that any clearer in these verses. The way of Jesus is the way of suffering. Until we can talk of significant ways in which we have denied ourselves in following Jesus, we should be wary of describing ourselves as his followers. Self-sacrifice has got to be the mark of following the one who sacrificed all that he had for us. It certainly used to be.

Self-Sacrifice for Self-Interest

So what have you denied yourself to follow Jesus? There must be something. If there's nothing, then you are not really following the Jesus who speaks to you here.

What is the suffering, what are the real crosses you have intentionally embraced because you are his disciple? Is it the painful distance between you and your non-Christian family because you now follow Jesus and keep trying to persuade them to follow him too? Is it a loving perseverance in a deeply unhappy marriage? Is it denying your children what their peers all enjoy so that gospel ministry can happen? For me it is (among other things) not having the sexual relationship with a man that I long for. I do that out of obedience to Jesus' words here.

All those things are hard. And so we all need plenty of motivation. Jesus' own experience of suffering should, perhaps, be more than enough to motivate us. But Jesus kindly provides us with even more: self-preservation.

> For whoever wants to save their life will lose it, but whoever loses their life for me and for the gospel will save it. What good is it for someone to gain the whole world, yet forfeit their soul? Or what can anyone give in exchange for their soul? (Mark 8:35–37)

Oddly the self-sacrifice that Jesus calls us to ends up not really being self-sacrifice at all. It is actually in our own best interests—in the long term. Take up your cross and it will be worth it in the end. Refuse to sacrifice something and you will lose everything in the end. Jesus is beginning a stark warning here—whether or not we follow his life of suffering is a great indicator of our eternal destiny. He continues:

> If anyone is ashamed of me and my words in this adulterous and sinful generation, the Son of Man will be ashamed of them when he comes in his Father's glory with the holy angels. (Mark 8:38)

Jesus puts things at their starkest here: when he returns to earth to judge, he will deny us if we have denied his words here. And we need to heed this warning because, to be honest, we are rather ashamed of Jesus' words here and in other places. We seem to have denied their application to us today. This is shown in how little this call to suffer like him features in either our evangelism or our discipleship courses. If it features at all, it is part of the very small print—not one of the first things we tell people once they have grasped who Jesus is. Here, in Jesus' own discipleship course, it is right at the start.

The result of this is an understandable incomprehension when the Christian life is actually quite hard work or when Jesus asks us to do hard things. That wasn't the deal, part of people's expectations. Jesus was meant to make their life better, not more difficult. So when suffering comes, that can't be Jesus' will for his people—surely he wants only what is best for them?

It's this new suffering-averse brand of Christianity that explains why few Christians in the West today are willing to face the grief that active evangelism brings, let alone to follow their forebears on to the mission field, persist in difficult marriages, give lifestyle-changing amounts of money away or say no to sex outside of marriage (as biblically defined). All this would involve Christlike self-sacrifice, and no one made it clear that that's what following him involves even today.

Living in the midst of this sort of Christianity obviously makes my choice to stay celibate as a same-sex attracted Christian sound so deeply implausible. The suffering that it inevitably brings confuses so many of my Christian contemporaries. It's changing the deal they signed up for. Like any consumers who didn't read the small print, they only want the offer they thought they were getting, which was suffering-free. So, of course, they rapidly transfer their allegiance to the churches and organizations that don't require Christians to embrace suffering.

So we need to check that the brand of Christianity we're both believing and sharing is the genuine article that Jesus articulates here in Mark 8—one that is centered on his self-sacrifice and that, in effect, defines his disciples as those willing to sacrifice themselves for him. We need to grasp the full danger that we run into when we stop clearly asking people to sacrifice personal happiness. In not asking people to stick to Jesus' costly commands about evangelism, married life, financial decisions or sexuality, we have (unintentionally) put their very salvation at stake. For we are not really following Jesus if we are not following the difficult path that he calls us to tread in these areas, having, of course, already trodden it himself.

I think the self-sacrifice involved in living my life as I am is the more plausibly Christian way than the alternative—which, if I ever followed it, would be fueled, most of all, by self-gratification.

Previous generations walked in Jesus' self-sacrificial way more consistently. And, of course, many Christians in non-

Western parts of the world today do—even a few in our own churches. They all help us see the plausibility of it in their Christian joy in the midst of their sufferings for Christ. When I most struggle with the plausibility of suffering for Jesus as a same-sex attracted Christian, I look at the much greater sufferings of the persecuted church and see that plausibility is proclaimed by the blood of the martyrs and the perseverance of the saints. I'm also reminded that it has always been those who are willing to suffer for Jesus who have been the most effective at attracting people to Jesus.

And, of course, it's not just in Mark 8 that true Christians are called to embrace Christlike self-sacrificial suffering. Jesus repeats the point elsewhere. Paul rarely writes a letter without both modeling and commending it. The Peter who rejected this suffering in Mark 8 proves he is no longer suffering-averse in his New Testament epistles. The expectation set by Jesus speaking to John in Revelation is one of continued suffering for his church until he returns and ends all suffering forever. Suffering cannot be avoided by those who follow him. It is part and parcel of the Christian life.

Why Suffering?

But why? Why on earth is there so much suffering in the life of any true Christian as long as they live on this earth? Why is God so wedded to it? Doesn't he know how painful it is? Yes, he does. In Jesus, he has experienced the worst of it.

But, as the death of Jesus shows, God has always used suffering to accomplish what is best for his people. And he's still using suffering to do the same today: to make his people more and more like Jesus.

Countless Christians have experienced the truth of this down the years. Converted slave-trader John Newton is just one:

I asked the Lord that I might grow
In faith, and love, and every grace;
Might more of His salvation know,
And seek, more earnestly, His face.

'Twas He who taught me thus to pray,
And He, I trust, has answered prayer!
But it has been in such a way,
As almost drove me to despair.

I hoped that in some favored hour,
At once He'd answer my request;
And by His love's constraining pow'r,
Subdue my sins, and give me rest.

Instead of this, He made me feel
The hidden evils of my heart;
And let the angry pow'rs of hell
Assault my soul in every part.

Yea more, with His own hand He seemed
Intent to aggravate my woe;
Crossed all the fair designs I schemed,
Blasted my gourds, and laid me low.

"Lord, why is this," I trembling cried,
"Wilt thou pursue thy worm to death?"
"'Tis in this way," the Lord replied,
"I answer prayer for grace and faith."

"These inward trials I employ,
From self, and pride, to set thee free;
And break thy schemes of earthly joy,
That thou may'st find thy all in Me."[1]

Newton prayed that he might become more like Jesus. God's answer to that prayer was for Newton to suffer like Jesus. And the logic there is impeccable—no one can become like another person without experiencing similar things to them. Any Christian who wants to become more and more like Christ will have to share in his sufferings.

All the Christians I most admire have become Christlike through suffering. For C. S. Lewis, it wasn't just the much-chronicled death of his wife after such a short marriage, but also his mother's death when he was a child, the loss of his best friend in the First World War, his long-term care of that friend's increasingly mentally ill mother and his own alcoholic brother that brought about the Christlike wisdom found in his books and letters. In my own church, the people I most want to be like (because they are most like Jesus) have become like him through great suffering. God has used forty years of chronic back pain in one woman's life to achieve the Christlikeness I covet.

And in my own life, as I've already shared, the thing that God has most used to make me more and more like Jesus is my experience of same-sex attraction. It's also been the thing that he has most used to equip me (as a pastor) to help others become more and more like Jesus too.

Some people might still be nervous of me claiming God has used something that is bad in his sight to bring about his good. But we need to remember that in Romans 8:28, he promises to use *all* things for the good of those who love him and whom he has called. We are wrong if we just want to limit those things to the good things in life; there is no such restriction in the text, and the rest of the Bible shows again and again God's ability to use all things—even human sin. Remember what Joseph said to his brothers about them selling him as a slave: "You intended to harm me, but God intended it for good to accomplish what is now being done, the saving of many lives" (Genesis 50:20). Recall how all the Old Testament greats (Abraham, Moses, David) were great sinners and yet how greatly God used them in (and through) their sins. Realize that your salvation depends on God being up for doing this; the cross was the greatest act of human sin ever and yet God used it to enable your sins to be forgiven.

In all church history, the group that best understood all this were the unjustly maligned Puritans. And so God has kindly used two of them to keep me from giving up on him when I suffer most because of my same-sex attraction. They have helped me to see how God has actually been using it all for my good, rather than as a bad thing that he has cruelly afflicted me with. I was, first of all, encouraged by these words of Thomas Brooks:

> God will so order the afflictions that befall you in the way of righteousness, that your souls shall say, We would not for all the world but that we had met with such and such troubles and afflictions: for surely, had not these befallen us, it would have been worse and worse with us. Oh the carnal security, pride, formality, dead-heartedness, luke-warmness, censoriousness, and earthliness that God hath cured us of, by the trouble and dangers that we have met with in the ways and services of the Lord![2]

These words could not be more true of me! Even with my experience of same-sex attraction, I am a comfort-seeking, proud, dutiful, cold-hearted, unfeeling, self-righteous and worldly Christian. It is the pain of my same-sex attraction that God has most effectively used to rid me slowly of these things—without it, they would have strangled me as a Christian. Brooks began to help me to be grateful for something I had up to then just been resentful about—to see God's (admittedly well-disguised) kindness to me.

John Flavel takes all of this, and so took me, a step further:

> It may support thy heart, to consider that in these troubles God is performing that work in which thy soul would rejoice, if thou didst see the design of it. We are clouded with much ignorance, and are not able to discern how particular providences tend to the fulfillment of God's designs; and therefore, like Israel in the wilderness, are often murmuring, because Providence leads us about in a howling desert, where we are exposed to difficulties; though he led, and is now leading us, *by the right way to a city of habitations.* If you could but see how God in his secret counsel has exactly laid the whole plan of your salvation, even to the smallest means and circumstances; could you but discern the admirable harmony of divine dispensations, their mutual relations, together with the general respect they all have to the last end; had you the liberty to make your own choice, you would, of all the conditions in the world, choose that in which you now are. Providence is like a curious piece of tapestry made of a thousand threads, which, single, appear useless, but put together, they represent, a beautiful history to the eye.[3]

Do you get his incredible point? The language is old, so I would suggest pausing and rereading it if that helps. His point is this: if I were in God's place (perish the thought)—with all wisdom and power at his disposal—I too would have permitted myself to experience same-sex attraction because of the good it will achieve in me. Something beautiful is, by his amazing grace, coming out of my suffering with it.

Scottish pastor Willie Still confirmed all of this from his own experience of pastoring people like me:

> I have known those who were faced with extreme temptation to "unnatural sin" who so resolutely refused to succumb to what fatally attracted them but which they knew was wrong, that I was astonished. But on reflection, I knew why their aesthetic, pastoral, and preaching gifts were signally used of God. That very drive, which could have ruined them was used, when transmogrified into an instrument of God, as the means of saving and blessing many.[4]

All of this helpful thinking presupposes that God is Lord over even our suffering and our sin (while still leaving us responsible for it, as we established earlier). Many are troubled by this (I think) clear biblical teaching. But it has actually comforted me more than almost any other teaching to know, with certainty, that my sexuality has been included, is being used, as part of God's perfect plan to make me (and, through me, others) more like Jesus. That makes my life choices seem plausible like nothing else. What a mistake we make when we think suffering is to be avoided!

I so often find myself back in 2 Corinthians 4 (the part of the Bible I want to be read at my funeral) and read wonderful verses like these:

> But we have this treasure in jars of clay to show that this all-surpassing power is from God and not from us. We are hard pressed on every side, but not crushed; perplexed, but not in despair; persecuted, but not abandoned; struck down, but not destroyed. We always carry around in our body the death of Jesus, so that the life of Jesus may also be

> revealed in our body. For we who are alive are always being
> given over to death for Jesus' sake, so that his life may also
> be revealed in our mortal body. So then, death is at work
> in us, but life is at work in you. (2 Corinthians 4:7-12)

I've yet to find a part of the Bible that better describes my life
experience, but which also articulates so well why it's worth it:
that God's power might be seen in my perseverance in the midst
of my sufferings, for the benefit of others and for his glory.
That's the sort of life Jesus lived for me; that's the life I want to
live for him.

And that is, as Jesus made clear in Mark 8, the authentic
Christian life, the life all those who follow him are to embrace:
suffering for the good purpose of becoming more and more like
him and so pointing more and more people to him. Make it
more plausible by ensuring that you are embracing it yourself.
But in doing so, never forget that any such suffering will be
worth it. C. S. Lewis wonderfully reminds us that

> any man who reaches Heaven will find that what he aban-
> doned (even in plucking out his right eye) has not been
> lost: that the kernel of what he was really seeking even in
> his most depraved wishes will be there, beyond expec-
> tation, waiting for him in "the High Countries."[5]

I'm looking forward to the joy that will be mine then. For the
right and lasting satisfaction of all my desires. And for the
eternal relief of a conversation with Jesus that will go something
like the one that King Caspian has with Aslan at the end of
Lewis's *The Silver Chair*:

> "Sir," said Caspian, "I've always wanted to have just one
> glimpse of their world. Is that wrong?"

"You cannot want wrong things any more, now that you
have died, my son," said Aslan.[6]

Not to be able even to *want* to do anything wrong anymore!
Imagine that for a moment; it moves me to tears every time I do.
How beautifully enjoyable that life in God's perfect new world
will be after a life of painful suffering in this God-rejecting old
one. Come Lord Jesus! Come soon and make "everything sad . . .
come untrue."[7]

Application Question

How can we help each other appreciate the good results of suffering in our lives?

Conclusion

Peter and Jane

It's time to return to Peter and Jane. Remember them? Peter is a young man exclusively attracted to his own sex. He's a sincere Christian, but is also sincere about wanting to have sex. Jane is a divorced, middle-aged woman who has recently begun a sexual relationship with another woman. She's an enthusiastic new Christian, but is also enthusiastic about her new relationship and the family life that it's brought her.

How can it be plausible to ask Peter to say no to sex forever, and to ask Jane to give up a relationship that has brought her so much joy? To continue to insist that the Bible's teaching is that sex is just for the marriage of a man and a woman, and that they should both remain single and celibate? This book has been all about making that sort of Christian life plausible to them, others like them, and the rest of us. How have we done?

At college, Peter will be encouraged to define as a gay man. Instead, I hope he will let God identify him as first and foremost a precious son of his, united to Jesus. I hope that Peter will come increasingly to recognize that his identity is in Christ and what Christ has done for him—not what his hormones do to him when a good-looking man walks past.

As Jane struggles to end her relationship because of the family life it has brought her, I trust that she will realize she's not waving goodbye to a family life forever. That whatever their failures, she has a family in the church that she is part of. They are her God-given, eternal family who really are there to share their lives with her and to walk with her to the end of her earthly life—and beyond.

I hope this book has given Peter the confidence to say that just because his same-sex attraction feels natural to him doesn't make it right. To point out that no one would use that reasoning when it comes to his innate selfishness or pride, and that his thinking and practice when it comes to his sexuality need to be shaped by the Bible's teaching on original sin.

When Jane is advised to do whatever makes her happy, I trust that she will now be rightly suspicious of anything that places a human definition of happiness in opposition to what her loving Father God guarantees will make her happy. That she will seek the lasting happiness that God's Word assures her belongs to those who trust in what God has said.

As Peter contemplates a sex-free life, I hope that he will now see that he's not signing up to a lonely life without any meaningful intimacy. That instead he's potentially going to enjoy *more* intimacy than many of his soon-to-be-married friends because he has more time and energy to invest in appropriately intimate friendships with members of both sexes than they do.

As Jane tries to get her mind around why God is so bothered about her sleeping with the woman who loves her, I trust that seeing marital sex as a divine trailer for the union in difference of Christ and the church will help her. That she will recognize that just as Christ and his church are not interchangeable, men and women aren't either. That it would be wrong to continue to desecrate this eternal picture of Jesus' love for the church.

When Peter's desperate prayers for his sexuality to change potentially go unanswered, and some counseling perhaps leaves his attraction to men undiminished, I hope that he will cling to the fact that godliness is not him stopping desiring men but becoming more and more like the man Jesus Christ. And that his loving Father God cares far more about the latter than the former.

For Jane, as she unwraps the gift of celibacy and wishes she had the receipt to return it, I trust that she will come to see it as a gift she's happy to keep. That it is more enjoyable and useful than she thought. That the single life was good enough for Jesus and so should be good enough for her too, bringing, as it did with him, great good into others' lives through her single-minded service.

For both Peter and Jane, as they sign up for lives of suffering, I hope that they will be encouraged to see that such self-sacrificial service is the hallmark of the Christian life. That it has been the mark of all the great Christians of the past and will make them great (in God's eyes) today. In fact, God will be using it, along with everything else in their lives, to make them (and others) more and more like him.

A Plausibility Structure

I don't know about you, but I think there's a plausibility structure there. Just typing all of that has encouraged me to keep going as a celibate, same-sex attracted Christian. It would seem to be a life worth living most fundamentally because it's a life that Jesus lived and has made liveable.

But they—and I—need your help. We same-sex attracted Christians can't build this plausibility structure by ourselves— you need to help us build it. And you need to recognize the many times when the church has (unintentionally) helped to destroy the very things that we needed, and will need, to help keep us living God's way.

So, if we fail to keep obeying God's Word, it will be your fault as well as ours. We will share the responsibility for that failure— unless you help the church to change in the various ways this book has proposed. You and your church need to start articulating and acting in the light of a whole number of key doctrines and truths that we have all neglected to pass on in recent years.

Each has been the focus of a chapter in this book: the pre-eminence of our union with Christ when it comes to forming our identity; the reality that church is our one everlasting family; the doctrine of original sin; the full authority and total goodness of God's Word; friendships, not just sex, bringing us all the human intimacy we need; marriage being all about the union of Christ and his church; godliness being all about Christlikeness, not who you are attracted to; the fact that singleness is truly a great gift; and the reality that following Jesus means taking up your cross and suffering like him.

To put it another way, we evangelicals are being called to be evangelicals again. To believe and do all the things our forebears have always believed and done when we've most made an impact on our world in the past. Read John Bunyan, William Wilberforce, Hannah More or Amy Carmichael, and you'll realize that they understood all of this. Listen to many evangelicals today, and you'll have to recognize that we've lost it.

We need to listen to pastor and scholar Henri Nouwen, who wrote:

> Many churches decorated with words announcing salvation and new life are often little more than parlors for those who feel quite comfortable in the old life, and who

are not likely to let the minister's words change their stone hearts into furnaces, where swords can be cast into plough-shares, and spears into pruning forks.[1]

Sadly, he could have been describing many evangelical churches today, churches that have settled for middle-class respectability rather than radical living for Jesus.

This means that instead of keeping very silent on the issue of homosexuality, hoping to avoid all of the controversy that it brings us, we should begin to see both the people who experience it and the controversy that it brings as a gift to the church. A divine gift, because it's just what we needed at this time in our history to help us see the whole series of tragic missteps we have taken to the detriment of us all, as well as to the detriment of the world we are trying to reach.

Throughout church history, wonderful theological clarity has come out of divisive theological controversy. Just a few names and times of conflict remind us of this: Athanasius and the early church councils, Martin Luther and the Reformation, Martin Luther King Jr. and the struggle for civil rights. So the current controversies over sexuality should excite rather than dismay us—it is from times of profound disagreement that our Sovereign God has often brought a return to a radical biblical clarity in the church's theology and practice.

And the debate on sexuality is especially exciting, because it touches on so many areas of theology and practice in which we have lost our biblical roots. Many of us have dreamed of a silver bullet that would solve many of the church's ills. We have, I believe, found it in this whole topic. Future generations could look back on us as gratefully as we look back on the eras of Athanasius, Martin Luther and Martin Luther King Jr.

That's why this plausibility problem matters so much. That's why we all need to pray and work hard to solve it. It's my hope and prayer that this book has made a small start—but it is only with your help that we'll finish. So what are *you* going to do about it *now*?

APPENDIX 1

The Plausibility of the Traditional Interpretation of Scripture

Back toward the beginning of this book I quoted the following words with approval. They summarize where I'm coming from so wonderfully that they are well worth quoting again:

> In the end, what keeps me on the path I've chosen is not so much individual proof texts from Scripture or the sheer weight of the church's traditional teaching against homosexual practice. Instead, it is, I think, those texts and traditions and teachings *as I see them from within the true story of what God has done in Jesus Christ*—and the whole perspective on life and the world that flows from that story, as expressed definitively in Scripture. Like a piece from a jigsaw puzzle finally locked into its rightful place, the Bible and the church's no to homosexual behavior make sense— it has the ring of truth, as J. B. Phillips once said of the New Testament—when I look at it as one piece within the larger Christian narrative. I abstain from homosexual behavior because of the power of the Scriptural story.[1]

I too abstain from homosexual practice because of the power of the timeless scriptural story.

But what story are we talking about? For me, it's the central plotline that I'm going to outline briefly now (what Hill calls "the true story of what God has done in Jesus Christ"). The Bible's metanarrative in its four great acts—creation, rebellion, redemption and perfection—all of them pointing us to Jesus. It is only in this big-picture context that the individual proof-texts make sense, so it is by seeing this wider vista that my choice can be seen as both right and plausible.

And, of course, no story makes any sense unless you start at the very beginning.

Act I: Creation

In the very beginning, we read of a good God who creates a good world. We read of him speaking night, sky, seas, trees, stars, eagles and cows into existence. And then we read:

> ²⁶Then God said, "Let us make mankind in our image, in our likeness, so that they may rule over the fish in the sea and the birds in the sky, over the livestock and all the wild animals, and over all the creatures that move along the ground."
>
> ²⁷So God created mankind in his own image,
>   in the image of God he created them;
>   male and female he created them.
>
> ²⁸God blessed them and said to them, "Be fruitful and increase in number; fill the earth and subdue it. Rule over the fish in the sea and the birds in the sky and over every living creature that moves on the ground." . . .

³¹God saw all that he had made, and it was very good.
And there was evening, and there was morning—the sixth
day. (Genesis 1:26-28, 31)

Here, at the beginning of the Bible's story, we have a few sentences that have supported the foundations of our view of ourselves and the world that we live in ever since. They have formed the basis of our understanding of anthropology, ecology and sexuality for numerous different cultures over many centuries. And when it comes to sexuality, they have always made a number of things crystal clear.

God created sexuality (Genesis 1:27) and sex (Genesis 1:28). God designed us as sexual beings. And so he's the authority on our gender and how it is best expressed. As our Creator, he has an authoritative perspective that no human traditions, cultures or feelings can ever better.

Sexuality and sex were part of God's perfect creation (Genesis 1:31). Christians have sometimes given the impression that sexuality and sex are part of what's gone wrong with God's good world. These verses undermine that view; God looked at the sexual beings he had created and pronounced them "very good."

All human beings are created in God's image (Genesis 1:27). Not just men. Not just women. But both, as misstep number six on gender explained. And someone's sexuality doesn't undermine this fact either: whoever God's image-bearers are found in bed with, it does not destroy their human status and dignity.

Men and women are different (Genesis 1:27). God created two different genders: male and female. Misstep number six on gender explains why, and here the simple fact is communicated. The biblical idea of equal status but different roles starts here, again before anything had gone wrong.

God wants men and women to have children (Genesis 1:28).
We can't ignore the clear link between the sexual difference articulated in verse 27 and the command God gives humanity in
verse 28. God needed the first if he was going to ask for the second.
But, as we've established, procreation still isn't the primary reason
for sexual difference—despite obviously demanding it.

The story continues in Genesis 2. But do you see how much
of a plausible sexual ethic is already in place? One that does
not require any human being to see their sexuality or sex as
intrinsically bad. One that does not dehumanize anyone because of who they might be attracted to or sleep with. One
that draws a clear distinction between the sexes and begins to
articulate why.

So let's read on into chapter 2 of Genesis, where a separate,
complementary creation narrative focuses our attention on
these human beings God has created. His special love and
concern for us is already clear:

> ¹⁸The Lord God said, "It is not good for the man to be
> alone. I will make a helper suitable for him."
>
> ¹⁹Now the Lord God had formed out of the ground all
> the wild animals and all the birds in the sky. He brought
> them to the man to see what he would name them; and
> whatever the man called each living creature, that was its
> name. ²⁰So the man gave names to all the livestock, the
> birds in the sky and all the wild animals.
>
> But for Adam no suitable helper was found. ²¹So the
> Lord God caused the man to fall into a deep sleep; and
> while he was sleeping, he took one of the man's ribs and
> then closed up the place with flesh. ²²Then the Lord God

made a woman from the rib he had taken out of the man, and he brought her to the man.

²³The man said,

> "This is now bone of my bones
>   and flesh of my flesh;
> she shall be called 'woman,'
>   for she was taken out of man."

²⁴That is why a man leaves his father and mother and is united to his wife, and they become one flesh.

²⁵Adam and his wife were both naked, and they felt no shame. (Genesis 2:18-25)

What does this part of the story tell us?

God does not want men and women to be alone (Genesis 2:18). The God who has eternally enjoyed life in the perfect community of the Trinity—Father, Son and Holy Spirit—is, unsurprisingly, not in favor of the man living alone. So he creates a community: not just another man, but a woman with the potential (through their sexual union) of creating a wider community too.

Marriage is between a man and a woman (Genesis 2:24). The only wedding with a simple guest list takes place soon after. And like the commentator at a royal wedding, the writer of Genesis makes sure that we don't miss the full significance of what has taken place (verse 24): what happened here is *the* blueprint for all the marriages that will follow. A gay "marriage" cannot fit that blueprint.

Marriage is sexual union (Genesis 2:24). You need a man and a woman, and they need to have sex. Marriage and sex are synonymous according to these verses. Talk of "one flesh" is about them becoming both a new family unit of kinship *and* one in their sexual union. That's why sex outside marriage is so wrong and damaging.

So, by the end of the second chapter, all the core biblical sexual ethics are in place. We are clearly told that marriage is for a man and a woman, and that sex is for marriage. God's parameters for me with my same-sex attraction are unambiguous. But they are not cruel—he does not want me to live life alone and has given me the same potential to live my life in community that he has given us all (and enjoys himself). That's a plausible life to me.

But is it really plausible to base our sex lives on a document written thousands of years ago in a very different culture? Surely we should change with the times? Why don't I? Because Jesus didn't. Listen to him answering a question about sex and relationships numerous years and cultures after Genesis was written:

> ²Some Pharisees came and tested him by asking, "Is it lawful for a man to divorce his wife?"
>
> ³"What did Moses command you?" he replied.
>
> ⁴They said, "Moses permitted a man to write a certificate of divorce and send her away."
>
> ⁵"It was because your hearts were hard that Moses wrote you this law," Jesus replied. ⁶"But at the beginning of creation God 'made them male and female.' ⁷'For this reason a man will leave his father and mother and be united to his wife, ⁸and the two will become one flesh.' So they are no longer two, but one flesh. ⁹Therefore what God has joined together, let no one separate." (Mark 10:2-9)

What's so striking about his answer?

Jesus treated Genesis as authoritative when asked about marriage (Mark 10:6-8). Jesus Christ is God incarnate; he had the authority and ability to articulate his own answer to this question about divorce. But what does he do? He takes us to Genesis 2 for an answer. He based his sexual ethics on the timeless truths of Genesis, despite all that had changed since then. We should always be eager to follow in his steps.

So I think it is eminently plausible to follow the traditional interpretation of the Scriptures when it comes to sexual ethics. If they are good enough for Jesus, they are good enough for me. Even more plausibility comes as the Bible's story continues.

Act II: Rebellion

If the Bible's story were being set to music, the second movement would switch to a minor key and we'd be hearing a lot from the largest drums in the orchestra. Come Genesis 3, it all goes wrong as the first man and woman break the one rule God had given them: not to eat from the tree of the knowledge of good and evil at the center of God's garden. We read:

> ⁶When the woman saw that the fruit of the tree was good for food and pleasing to the eye, and also desirable for gaining wisdom, she took some and ate it. She also gave some to her husband, who was with her, and he ate it. ⁷Then the eyes of both of them were opened, and they realized they were naked; so they sewed fig leaves together and made coverings for themselves.
>
> ⁸Then the man and his wife heard the sound of the LORD God as he was walking in the garden in the cool of the day, and they hid from the LORD God among the trees of the garden. ⁹But the LORD God called to the man, "Where are you?"
>
> ¹⁰He answered, "I heard you in the garden, and I was afraid because I was naked; so I hid." (Genesis 3:6-10)

What do we learn from this act of open rebellion against the God who had made them and given them his good world?

Humanity made the decision to reject God's Word (Genesis 3:6). At the heart of all that is wrong with this world is a decision that humankind made: Adam and Eve's joint decision to disobey God, having doubted his goodness (see Genesis 3:1-5). They acted as the rest of humanity's representative on that day and did that job well: they did exactly what we would have done if we'd been there instead.

All human relationships are marred (Genesis 3:7). There had been nothing between Adam and Eve—literally. No "Does my bum look big in this?" because they wore no clothes. But now that question would have been asked for the first time: all the embarrassment and shame about human bodies goes back to this day. But so does everything else that comes between human beings.

All sexual relationships are marred (Genesis 3:7). There has been no perfect sexual relationship since then. Even the "perfect" heterosexual Christian couple who keep sex for marriage have plenty to be ashamed of and embarrassed about their sexuality and their use of it. When I share those feelings of imperfection as a same-sex attracted Christian, I should not be made to feel alone.

Humanity's relationship with God is marred (Genesis 3:8-10). The most pointless game of hide-and-seek ever (and there is plenty of competition) represents how humanity's relationship with God has gone wrong. They used to enjoy each other's company—now humanity runs away from their Creator.

And the full implications of this rebellion are spelled out not only as God catches up with them in the rest of the chapter but as the results catch up with humanity for the rest of the Bible's story.

The apostle Paul was just reflecting on these consequences when he wrote these infamous words in the opening chapter of his letter to the Christian church in Rome:

> ²⁴Therefore God gave them over in the sinful desires of their hearts to sexual impurity for the degrading of their bodies with one another. ²⁵They exchanged the truth about God for a lie, and worshiped and served created things rather than the Creator—who is forever praised. Amen.
>
> ²⁶Because of this, God gave them over to shameful lusts. Even their women exchanged natural sexual relations for unnatural ones. ²⁷In the same way the men also abandoned natural relations with women and were inflamed with lust for one another. Men committed shameful acts with other men, and received in themselves the due penalty for their error. (Romans 1:24-27)

We should read these verses not as a condemnation of specific sexual excess in Rome, or of heterosexuals acting like homosexuals (two recent interpretations), but as it has traditionally been understood: as a commentary on Genesis 3. Having studied both texts carefully, biblical scholar Morna Hooker concludes, "It would appear from this remarkable parallelism that Paul's account of man's wickedness has been deliberately stated in terms of the narrative of Adam's fall."[2] Paul is condemning not specific time-sensitive situations but the human idolatry (worshiping created things rather than the Creator) that has been humanity's default position since Genesis 3 (with homosexual sex as his working example).

So, set in the context of the Bible's big picture, these verses are no longer just an isolated proof-text but part of Paul's interpretation and application of a central episode in the main story. The Christian church throughout history has therefore been right to use them to conclude that . . .

Same-sex sexual relationships are wrong (Romans 1:26-27). At all times, and in all contexts. New Testament expert Simon Gathercole summarizes Paul's argument here well:

> *Humanity* should be orientated toward *God* but turns in on itself (Rom. 1.25).
>
> *Woman* should be oriented toward *man*, but turns in on itself (Rom. 1.26).
>
> *Man* should be oriented toward *woman*, but turns in on itself (Rom. 1.27).[3]

Same-sex sexual activity is one sadly brilliant example of all human rebellion against God—getting us worshiping ourselves, on our own terms, rather than worshipping the God who made us, on his.

Do you see how all of this helps me to see the plausibility of the traditional interpretation of Scripture when it comes to homosexuality? It's not an insignificant detail that doesn't matter very much or about which God has changed his mind. Instead, it is one of the best examples that can be found of human idolatry. It's big and still bad.

At one level, this makes me feel bad—I practice one of the best (and so worst!) forms of idolatry. That's humbling. But in Paul's argument (and throughout the rest of the Bible), it is just *one* example of idolatry—plenty of which I don't practice but you do. Just so you're kept humble too.

By now, the moody music has begun to get on our nerves and we want the story to take a turn for the better. Thankfully, it does.

Act III: Redemption

I love these words from the beginning of Sally Lloyd-Jones's *The Jesus Storybook Bible*:

> Now some people think the Bible is a book of rules, telling you what you should and shouldn't do. The Bible certainly does have some rules in it. They show you how life works best. But the Bible isn't mainly about you and what you should be doing. It is about God and what he has done.
>
> Other people think the Bible is a book of heroes, showing you people you should copy. The Bible does have some heroes in it, but (as you'll soon find out) most of the people in the Bible aren't heroes at all. They all make some big mistakes (some on purpose). They get afraid and run away. At times they are downright mean.
>
> No, the Bible isn't a book of rules, or a book of heroes. The Bible is most of all a Story. It's an adventure story about a young Hero who comes from a far country to win back his lost treasure. It's a love story about how a brave Prince who leaves his palace, his throne—everything—to rescue the one he loves. It's like the most wonderful of fairy tales that has come true in real life!
>
> You see the best thing about this Story is—it's true.[4]

By the end of Genesis 3, humanity's need of this rescuing prince has been both made clear *and* promised (Genesis 3:15). And that rescue, as Lloyd-Jones wonderfully points out, is the focus of the rest of the Bible's true story—repeatedly trailed throughout the rest of the Old Testament and then wonderfully fulfilled in the incarnation, crucifixion, resurrection and ascension of the God-man Jesus Christ.

The apostle Paul explains how Jesus carried out this rescue in these verses from Romans 3:

²¹But now apart from the law the righteousness of God has been made known, to which the Law and the Prophets testify. ²²This righteousness is given through faith in Jesus Christ to all who believe. There is no difference between Jew and Gentile, ²³for all have sinned and fall short of the glory of God, ²⁴and all are justified freely by his grace through the redemption that came by Christ Jesus. ²⁵God presented Christ as a sacrifice of atonement, through the shedding of his blood—to be received by faith. He did this to demonstrate his righteousness, because in his forbearance he had left the sins committed beforehand unpunished—²⁶he did it to demonstrate his righteousness at the present time, so as to be just and the one who justifies those who have faith in Jesus. (Romans 3:21-26)

God's spokesman makes it very clear:

All are sinners (Romans 3:23). All human beings need Jesus to rescue them from their sins. Paul has spent the previous three chapters showing that this was true of both Jew and Gentile. He would happily assent to the idea that it is true of both heterosexuals and homosexuals (and anyone in between).

All can be made right with God through faith in Jesus (Romans 3:24). No one is excluded. Note how emphatic both verses 23 *and* 24 are. Jews can be rescued by Jesus—so can Gentiles. Heterosexuals can be rescued by Jesus—so can homosexuals. Trust in Jesus (verses 22, 25 and 26) is all that is needed to become right in God's sight—through his death in our place on the cross.

So all I need to do is to trust in Jesus to forgive me—and then get on and live my life as I want? That's a mistake that Christians have kept making down the centuries; Paul had to correct that sort of thinking and behavior in first-century Corinth.

> ⁹Or do you not know that wrongdoers will not inherit the kingdom of God? Do not be deceived: Neither the sexually immoral nor idolaters nor adulterers nor men who have sex with men ¹⁰nor thieves nor the greedy nor drunkards nor slanderers nor swindlers will inherit the kingdom of God. ¹¹And that is what some of you were. But you were washed, you were sanctified, you were justified in the name of the Lord Jesus Christ and by the Spirit of our God. (1 Corinthians 6:9-11)

Here Paul is helping Christians then (and now) come to appreciate that . . .

Some patterns of behavior put you outside God's kingdom (1 Corinthians 6:9-10). There are patterns of behavior that, if you do not repent of them, show you're not part of God's kingdom. To keep on doing the things in this long list of sinful behaviors (homosexual sex being one among many) is inconsistent with a claim to be a follower of Jesus. We can't just do what we want to: we now belong to him (as Paul will go on to argue).

There have always been homosexual Christians (1 Corinthians 6:11). Note that these verses make it clear that there have always been Christians who were, as we would put it, "gay." The early churches were just like our churches today because they were in cities just like our cities today—where almost every type of sexual practice was on display.

Christianity changes your identity permanently (1 Corinthians 6:11). Verse 11 is why I don't describe myself as gay—it makes it clear that a Christian's fundamental identity is rooted not in his or her behavior or feelings but in God's behavior toward him or her. In the fact that our great triune God has transformed us into those now capable (clean, holy, sinless) of enjoying everlasting fellowship.

All of this makes the Jesus way seem very plausible to me. I (like everyone else) am called a sinner. But (like everyone else) I'm offered forgiveness for my sins—Jesus will graciously take God's right punishment for me. As a result (like every other Christian), it's now just as if I'd never sinned. So I (like every other Christian) am not to keep on sinning—that is inconsistent with my new status. I'm not discriminated against because of my sexuality. God treats me exactly the same way as he treats all his children. Which means I'm very much looking forward to the final part of the story.

Act IV: Perfection

This, of course, is what we were created for in the very first place. C. S. Lewis writes of

> our lifelong nostalgia, our longing to be reunited with something in the universe from which we now feel cut off, to be on the inside of some door which we have always seen from the outside, is no mere neurotic fancy, but the truest index of our real situation.
>
> At present we are on the outside of the world, the wrong side of the door. We discern the freshness and purity of the morning, but they do not make us fresh and pure. We cannot mingle with the splendors we see. But all the leaves of the New Testament are rustling with the rumor that it will not always be so. Some day, God willing, we shall get *in*.[5]

One day soon, all those who have trusted in God's rescuing hero Jesus will be let into God's perfectly restored creation: the world we've always wanted because it's the world for which we were created.

And, interestingly, this will be a world in which people do not marry. In answer to a question about bodily resurrection, Jesus himself tells us that "when the dead rise, they will neither marry nor be given in marriage; they will be like the angels in heaven" (Mark 12:25). So . . .

Marriage and sex are temporary (Mark 12:25). The be all and end all of many people's lives here on earth is not the be all and end all of life in God's new creation. Marriage vows made until "death us do part" have set the right best-before date for marriage: it is ended by death.

Why? Because you no longer need to watch the trailer when the film itself has been released. We shall then be experiencing the eternal marriage to which all the others have (with differing degrees of success) been pointing us. This will be our experience then.

> [1]Then I saw "a new heaven and a new earth," for the first heaven and the first earth had passed away, and there was no longer any sea. [2]I saw the Holy City, the new Jerusalem, coming down out of heaven from God, prepared as a bride beautifully dressed for her husband. [3]And I heard a loud voice from the throne saying, "Look! God's dwelling place is now among the people, and he will dwell with them. They will be his people, and God himself will be with them and be their God. [4]'He will wipe every tear from their eyes. There will be no more death' or mourning or crying or pain, for the old order of things has passed away."
>
> [5]He who was seated on the throne said, "I am making everything new!" Then he said, "Write this down, for these words are trustworthy and true."
>
> [6]He said to me: "It is done. I am the Alpha and the

Omega, the Beginning and the End. To the thirsty I will give water without cost from the spring of the water of life. [7]Those who are victorious will inherit all this, and I will be their God and they will be my children. [8]But the cowardly, the unbelieving, the vile, the murderers, the sexually immoral, those who practice magic arts, the idolaters and all liars—they will be consigned to the fiery lake of burning sulfur. This is the second death." (Revelation 21:1-8)

This vision that Jesus gave his friend John helps us to understand a number of important truths.

In the new creation, the whole church will be married to Jesus (Revelation 21:2). There will be no single people in heaven—no lonely Valentine's Days—but instead one great eternal relationship of love that we will all be bound up in and celebrating together forever.

Marriage to Jesus will be better than sex (Revelation 21:3-4). I hear that sex can be great. But if I die a virgin, I will not be missing out: the eternal consummation of my relationship with Jesus will be far better that the temporary consummation of any human relationships. The latter always leads to death and mourning and crying and pain; the former will bring nothing but lasting joy.

This perfect marriage is open to all (Revelation 21:6-7). Although it qualifies as a royal wedding, there is no highly restricted invitation list: anyone who RSVPs to the invitation to drink Jesus' water of life will be there at the wedding breakfast. And there all that they have rightly thirsted for will be satisfied by him.

But it can be rejected (Revelation 21:8). Access is not for all: sinful attitudes and actions that you haven't repented of (including sex outside marriage) mean you won't get in. Those who haven't turned to Jesus for forgiveness of their unbelief and self-centered behavior will experience a destructive eternity without him and any of the good things he would have given them.

Won't my life choices seem eminently sensible then? Eternity with Jesus because of a life spent trusting in his words and repenting of my sins—rather than an eternity without him because of a life spent distrusting his words and rejoicing in my sins? I'm not going to be kicking myself for my lack of a sex life in the painful past as I enjoy life in the perfect future! I'm not going to be asking God for my money back as I feast with him forever. I'm going to be enjoying *perfection*: mine is going to be a story that will end well.

So do you get the plausibility of the traditional interpretation of Scripture? How, in the light of the big story of the Bible, the ban on gay sex makes sense and my life of celibacy is right for me, as well as anyone else who experiences exclusive same-sex attraction? One sentence from the apostle Paul draws it all together for me: "The life I now live in the body, I live by faith in the Son of God, who loved me and gave himself for me" (Galatians 2:20). In the light of his loving rescue of me, it makes complete sense to trust in God's Word, as Jesus himself did, and not change our minds about what the church has always taught down the ages. It's the only plausible way to live.

APPENDIX 2

The Implausibility of the New Interpretations of Scripture

But what about the other side? Surely the rejection of the traditional interpretation of Scripture has been fueled by some highly plausible new interpretations of Scripture. You might have thought so. But in reading the recent books of Jeffrey John (dean of St. Albans Abbey), Justin Lee (executive director of the Gay Christian Network), James Brownson (professor of New Testament at the Western Theological Seminary in Michigan) and Matthew Vines (president of the Reformation Project), true plausibility is the main thing missing. Although all claim to take the Bible seriously (and all, apart from John, share an evangelical heritage), they all consistently fail to do so. If you think I'm being harsh, read them for yourself in light of what I've written below.

But if they are so wrong, why have their books and arguments been increasingly successful? Well, there are three chief weapons that I think they each deploy with expert skill.

1. Emotion

We all like to pretend that our decisions are primarily driven by rational thinking, but advertisers and pollsters know that it is our emotions that drive us. The revisionist writers on sexuality have grasped this too and keep pulling on their readers' heartstrings.

Personal narrative is (as I demonstrated with Peter and Jane) the most effective way of doing this. And you'd have to be very cold-hearted not to be moved by Lee's account of coming to terms with his sexuality, Vines's painful conversations with his dad or Brownson's raw response to his son coming out as gay. They all communicate so effectively the anguish that this issue can bring for individuals, families and churches.

I know because I've shared that pain; I don't want to diminish theirs. But, however distressing the story, we need to resist the temptation to let personal experience trump revealed truth: this is a contemporary habit, but it is not the way to reconstruct Christian ethics.

Neither is the sort of emotive language they all deploy at times. Matthew Vines provides us with a good example:

> No other teaching that Christians widely continue to embrace has caused anything like the torment, destruction, and alienation from God that the church's rejection of same-sex relationships has caused. If we tell people that their *every* desire for intimate, sexual bonding is shameful and disordered, we encourage them to hate a core part of who they were created to be. And if we reject the desires of gay Christians to express their sexuality within a lifelong covenant, we separate them from our covenantal God, and we tarnish their ability to bear his image.[1]

Notice the sweeping, negative language used here—if this were true, it would be appalling. Note too how some of the idols of our age (sexual intimacy, individual expression) are appealed to effectively. Reading these words, it is hard not to recoil from what is being portrayed as the church's traditional teaching; but when its biblical sexual ethics are understood and applied rightly, none of this is actually right or true.

So, when reading any of the revisionist texts, please be aware of when your emotions are being played on. And of how these emotions will be intensified by . . .

2. Polarization

In most political campaigns today, each side does their best to push their opponents to the extremes so that they themselves can be seen to occupy the center ground. This is skilfully done by Brownson and Vines in particular. Again, Matthew Vines provides us with the best example:

> For straight Christians, abstinence affirms the goodness both of marriage and of sex within marriage. But for gay Christians, mandatory celibacy affirms something different: the sinfulness of every possible expression of their sexuality.[2]

Do you see what he's doing? Saying that Christians like me (who encourage same-sex attracted Christians to remain celibate) are being totally unreasonable in insisting that every possible expression of homosexuality is bad. But I'm not: as I've made clear in this book, there are many aspects and expressions of my sexuality that I can and do rightly affirm (how it helps me grasp God's love for me, how it's been used to make me more and more like Jesus, and so much else). My perspective on my same-sex attraction is in no way as negative as he portrays it, but it obviously helps his argument to push me to an extreme. Such polarization is a useful rhetorical device, but it doesn't accurately reflect the biblically nuanced case that people like me are trying to make. Instead, it just creates a black-and-white distinction in which Vines increases his chances of being seen as right.

So if you ever read one of the revisionist texts, please be aware that they may not be articulating the traditional view accurately. And, also, how much they rely on simply creating . . .

3. Doubt

Justin Lee is the master of this. He rightly affirms the importance of Scripture, but his chapter looking at the biblical texts on homosexual sex delivers no knock-out blow to the traditional interpretations, just a lot of questions. He concludes:

> And so, it seemed, the entire Bible argument came down to this one word. The Leviticus and Romans passages had a clear context of idolatry, not committed relationship. If 1 Corinthians 6:9 was condemning the same things, or something else like pederasty, then the Bible didn't address committed gay relationships at all. If *arsenokoitai*, however, was really a reference to all gay sex in every time and place, then it shed light on other passages as well, and any other interpretation was just looking for loopholes.
>
> I realized with frustration that neither answer was entirely satisfactory. I could make an argument for either side, but whatever argument I made, how did I know I was right? If I got this wrong, I'd end up either trying to justify sin or unjustly condemning loving relationships that God never intended to condemn.
>
> I tried reading the passage one way. Then I tried the other. They both sounded convincing, yet they both left me feeling thoroughly unconvinced.[3]

It is hard for Lee's doubts not to become infectious when they are written up in this kind of way. Once you've said that the entire biblical position on homosexuality comes down to one word, and we can't be sure what that word means, anyone's doubts run riot. We do then seem free to build our own sexual ethic (which is what Lee goes on to do). But the entire biblical argument does *not* come down to one word. As appendix one made clear, the argument is based on the entire story of the Bible. But that argument is completely ignored by Justin Lee, who seems to prefer articulating the doubts and questions that then allow him to make up his own mind.

So you need to be aware of the power of doubts as you read the revisionist authors: "Did God really say?" is their constant refrain, and that has always been a dangerous question. They subtly attack God's authority and undermine his goodness, in ways that were first used a long time ago—with devastating effect.

But why do the revisionists have to depend so much on emotion, polarization and doubt? Because they cannot convincingly use the one weapon that matters: the Bible (Hebrews 4:12). Despite their claim to take the Scriptures seriously, they consistently break some of the most basic rules of biblical interpretation. Let me give you just a few examples.

1. They Don't Interpret Passages in Their Full Biblical Theological Context

Near the beginning of his book, James Brownson encouragingly writes, "We do not interpret rightly any single passage of Scripture until we locate the text within this larger fabric of meaning in Scripture as a whole."[4] But this is something that he and the other revisionists consistently fail to do. Their focus is nearly always on the proof-texts in isolation, rather than the larger biblical theology of marriage or sin or, indeed, anything.

They also don't understand the Old Testament in the light

of the New. The weak argument that because Christians now eat shrimp, we can trash the whole of Leviticus, ignores both Jesus' high view of the law (Matthew 5:17-20) and the fact that it rightly took explicit teaching from him to change his people's eating habits (Mark 7:18-19), but Jeffrey John still uses it.[5] The light that Jude 7 throws on some of the sins of Sodom is simply ignored.

They don't understand the New Testament in the light of the Old either. Difficult New Testament passages are so often understood fully when you grasp the Old Testament background. So New Testament scholars like Morna Hooker and Simon Gathercole (coming from very different theological perspectives) are right to seek clarity on the big picture of Romans 1 in Genesis 3 (Hooker)[6] and Numbers 11 (Gathercole)[7] rather than extrabiblical sources. This is another classic mistake that the revisionist authors make.

2. They Rely Too Heavily on Extrabiblical Sources

For the revisionists, the key to understanding Romans 1 is not found in the Bible (despite the clear links back to Genesis 3 and Numbers 11), but in, to take one example, the sexual excess of the court of the Emperor Caligula (despite the lack of any clear link in the text).[8] Contemporary historical research is raided to justify a totally new interpretation.

Jeffrey John even descends to theology by innuendo, when he writes this about the Roman centurion and his servant whom we meet in Matthew 8:5-13 and Luke 7:1-10: "Any Jew encountering them, or reading the Gospel story about them, would almost certainly have assumed they were gay lovers."[9] From this doubtful supposition, with no warrant in the biblical text, we are meant to reinterpret the incident as indi-

cating Jesus' apparent approval of their same-sex sexual relationship[10]—although (even if they were in one) Jesus'
interactions with, say, tax-collectors and prostitutes are never
interpreted to include his approval of their corrupt lifestyles.

Now, extrabiblical sources can and do obviously inform
our biblical interpretation, but to let them *determine* it is very
dangerous. We become reliant on the latest PhD to hear God
correctly, rather than seeking to understand his words in
front of us in their original biblical context. You'd have to take
a degree in ancient history before you can understand things
for yourself.

A final example of this sort of bad biblical interpretation is that . . .

3. They Set Scripture Against Scripture

I am, for my sins, an Anglican. Article XX of *The Thirty-Nine
Articles of Religion* of the Church of England is titled "Of the
Authority of the Church" and says this:

> The Church hath power to decree Rites or Ceremonies, and
> authority in Controversies of Faith: And yet it is not lawful
> for the Church to ordain any thing that is contrary to God's
> Word written, *neither may it so expound one place of
> Scripture, that it may be repugnant to another.* Wherefore,
> although the Church be a witness and a keeper of holy
> Writ, yet, as it ought not to decree anything against the
> same, so besides the same ought it not to enforce anything
> to be believed for necessity of Salvation.[11]

The italics are mine and are the words that I want you to reg-
ister—so don't worry if you don't follow the rest of the sixteenth-
century language. They articulate a key principle of how to read
the Bible: we shouldn't explain one bit of Scripture in a way that

contradicts another, perhaps by teaching one verse in a way that completely undermines a verse in another part of the Bible. If two parts of the Bible seem to contradict each other, you have to hold them in a creative tension—rather than ignoring the one you like least.

This is a key principle that the revisionists seem to have rejected. So for James Brownson, Paul's words articulating Christian equality in Galatians 3:27-28 trump all the other passages that stress any difference. The different gender roles set out in passages like Ephesians 5:22-33 are bound by time and space, but the equality trumpeted in Galatians is for all times and places. Brownson contends:

> Throughout the history of Christianity the eschatological vision of Galatians 3:27-28 has slowly but surely undermined patriarchal structures and relationships, as well as those between masters and slaves, so that more and more, the church has begun to experience in its daily life its destiny as the new creation, where there is "no longer Jew or Greek, no longer slave or free, no longer male and female, for you are all one in Christ Jesus."[12]

The problem is that he produces no real evidence that these words from one of Paul's earliest letters were meant to supersede what he wrote in some of his later ones. Or why they are forever, and his other teaching in this area can be thrown out. He is expounding one part of Scripture in a way that just doesn't fit with a number of other parts.

Rather than working out the creative tension between equality and difference, he edits away those parts of God's Word that aren't convenient to his argument and modern life today. That is a wrong thing to do.

Last Words

I could go on and critique the revisionists' very attitude to Scripture, their bad understanding of key passages like 1 Corinthians 7, and much, much more, but it is time to draw all of this together. And I think I can do so by quoting a gay, atheist journalist.

London Times columnist Matthew Parris wrote these words back in 2003, when one of these revisionist authors (Jeffrey John) had been nominated as a bishop in the Church of England. Parris wanted to ask people like them and him:

> Can they honestly say that they would have drawn from Christ's teaching the same lessons of sexual tolerance in 1000, or 1590, or indeed 1950? Surely not, for almost no such voices were heard then.
>
> In which case, to what does this "reform" amount? Like changes to Church teaching on divorce or Sunday observance, the new tolerance gains its force within the Anglican Communion from a fear of becoming isolated from changing public morals. Is that a reason for a Christian to modify his own morality? I cannot recall that Moses took this view of golden calf worship. Whispering beneath the modernisers' soft aspirational language of love and tolerance, I hear an insistent "when in Rome, we must do as the Romans do. Times have changed." Gays in particular should be very wary of that message; some of us remember when it was used against us, and such a time may come again.
>
> A religion needs a compass. Logic alone does not point the way and religion adds to the general stock of human reasonableness a new directional needle—if it adds anything at all. I cannot read the Gospels in any way other than as declaring that this was revealed to man by God through

Jesus. Revelation, therefore, not logic, must lie at the core of the Church's message. You cannot pick and choose from revealed truth.[13]

He articulates what is essentially wrong with what the revisionists are attempting: picking and choosing from revealed truth (the Bible). Their tragedy is that they will end up with a tame idol of their own making, a Tashlan[14] who says and does what they want him to, rather than a plausible lion of a God, who is not tame, but instead says and does what he wants *us* to do. I know which one I'd prefer to live my life for.

Acknowledgments

In writing this book, I've often been comforted by Flannery O'Connor's words that "all writing is painful and . . . if it is not painful then it is not worth doing."[1] Writing about one of my areas of greatest weakness and failure has been very tough at times, so I've been kept going by the sort of hope she offers. I trust and pray that you feel it has been worth it.

This book has also been eased into life by the prayers, help and encouragement of many people that I need to thank now. But rather than compiling a long list of the many individuals who have made it possible, I want to thank a few groups: then I (hopefully!) won't offend anyone by leaving their name out.

First, I need to thank the team at IVP for taking on and helping out a new author who wanted to publish something on one of the most controversial topics the church is facing today.

I also need to thank the whole team behind Living Out (www.livingout.org), who first got me writing on this subject. I'm especially grateful to my fellow editorial team members who have given me input from their lives on the inside of this issue. Their companionship has been one of the chief joys of the last couple of years.

The number of notes at the end of this book highlights how much my thinking has been shaped by countless others, and I'm very grateful to all those whose writing has shaped my attitudes and actions in profound ways.

My church family at Emmanuel Bristol have wonderfully turned a blind eye to how much of my time working for them has been used on this book and Living Out. Their love and care for me are so often despite my preoccupation and busyness on other things—I hope that all of them, especially the church I now pastor (Emmanuel City Centre), will see more of me from now on.

All those who have read this book in various drafts deserve a special mention for keeping me going when I was (on countless occasions) about to give up. I think about twenty strangers and friends have improved things in countless ways with insightful (and humorous) comments—any faults that remain are, of course, entirely down to me.

I hope that one of the impressions this book has given is that my life has been incredibly blessed by my friends and family. Any such impression would be an accurate one. My friends are incredibly patient with me as I slowly learn to be the sort of friend they are for me. My family are kindly indulgent of me, the strange life I've chosen and the one-off person I am ("Silly Uncle Ed," as my eldest nephew and niece constantly label me).

I've dedicated this book to my parents, Jonathan and Hazel Shaw. I need to thank them not just for my life as their child but for my eternal life as God's child too. They are the people whom God has most used to help me see why and how we should follow Jesus. They've bred in me a love for him (and books!) that has made me the person I am today. I am, and always will be, eternally grateful to them and him.

Recommended Reading

If you want further help in seeking to solve the plausibility problem, the titles below would be the top ten books that anybody could—and everybody should—read. They are in alphabetical order (just in case Sam is too encouraged).

Allberry, Sam. *Is God Anti-Gay? And Other Questions About Homosexuality, the Bible and Same-Sex Attraction*. London: The Good Book Company, 2013.

A short and readable book that faithfully and clearly answers all the basic questions people have about God and this issue.

Brooks, Thomas. *Precious Remedies Against Satan's Devices*. Edinburgh: Banner of Truth, 1984.

Brooks beats C. S. Lewis's *The Screwtape Letters* in its insightful and practical help for the daily battle against sin, the world and the devil.

Chester, Tim, and Steve Timmis. *Everyday Church: Mission by Being Good Neighbours*. Nottingham, UK: Inter-Varsity Press, 2011.

If you want to think through how your church can be the sort of radical and attractive community that all can feel part of, this is the book to read.

Hill, Wesley. *Washed and Waiting: Reflections on Christian Faithfulness and Homosexuality*. Grand Rapids: Zondervan, 2010.

Want to know what it feels like to be a same-sex attracted Christian man? Hill has beautifully written what is, for me, the definitive account.

Keller, Timothy, with Kathy Keller. *The Meaning of Marriage: Facing the Complexities of Commitment with the Wisdom of God.* New York: Riverhead, 2011.

The best book on marriage, because it is biblically faithful and well applied—to both marrieds and singles.

Paul, Ian. *Same-Sex Unions: The Key Biblical Texts.* Cambridge: Grove Books, 2014.

This short booklet is the best introductory guide to what the Bible teaches, from a scholar who interacts well with the latest revisionist arguments.

Roberts, Vaughan. *True Friendship: Walking Shoulder to Shoulder.* Leyland, UK: 10Publishing, 2013.

This short and practical booklet on friendship challenges us all to build the friendships we need in order to thrive as human beings.

Tylee, Alex. *Walking with Gay Friends: A Journey of Informed Compassion.* Nottingham, UK: Inter-Varsity Press, 2007.

Tylee both shares her experience of same-sex attraction and helps Christians grasp how they can be supportive.

West, Christopher. *Fill These Hearts: God, Sex and the Universal Longing.* New York: Image, 2012.

West provides the best explanation of the reasons behind God's creation of marriage and sex, and how these truths should impact us today.

Wharton, Kate. *Single-Minded: Being Single, Whole and Living Life to the Full.* Oxford: Monarch, 2013.

The best book on singleness, because she is so honestly helpful about living the single life today, giving its advantages as well as the downsides.

Notes

Chapter 1: The Plausibility Problem

[1]Doctrinal Basis of the Universities and Colleges Christian Fellowship (UCCF), www.uccf.org.uk/about/doctrinal-basis.htm (accessed August 30, 2014).

[2]Melinda Selmys, "Sad Bad Sex," Sexual Authenticity blog, last modified April 27, 2013, http://sexual authenticity.blogspot.co.uk/2013/04/sad -bad-sex.html.

Chapter 2: The Plausibility Problem and Me

[1]Evelyn Waugh's beautiful novel that chronicles the homoerotic friendship of two Oxford students—one of whom then goes on to have an affair with the other's sister.

[2]Wesley Hill, *Washed and Waiting: Reflections on Christian Faithfulness and Homosexuality* (Grand Rapids: Zondervan, 2010), 61.

[3]Russell D. Moore, *Tempted and Tried: Temptation and the Triumph of Christ* (Wheaton, IL: Crossway, 2011), 89.

Misstep #1: "Your identity is your sexuality."

[1]See Ritch C. Savin-Williams, *The New Gay Teenager* (Cambridge, MA: Harvard University Press, 2005), 8-9, for a secular case for using the term "same-sex attraction."

[2]Kevin DeYoung, *The Hole in Our Holiness: Filling the Gap between Gospel Passion and the Pursuit of Godliness* (Wheaton, IL: Crossway, 2012), 100.

[3]Matthew Mason, "Reorienting Our Sex Talk," Theopolis Institute, last modified June 19, 2013, https://theopolisinstitute.com/reorienting-our -sex-talk.

[4]For examples of this slightly different approach, see the excellent spiritualfriendship.org.

[5]Russell D. Moore, *Tempted and Tried: Temptation and the Triumph of Christ* (Wheaton, IL: Crossway, 2011), 72.

[6]Mark A. Yarhouse, *Homosexuality and the Christian: A Guide for Parents, Pastors, and Friends* (Bloomington, MN: Bethany House, 2010), 54.

Misstep #2: "A family is mom, dad and 2.4 children."

[1]Alex Davidson, *The Returns of Love: A Christian View of Homosexuality* (Nottingham, UK: Inter-Varsity Press, 1970), 16.

[2]John Piper, *This Momentary Marriage: A Parable of Permanence* (Wheaton, IL: Crossway, 2009), 111.

Misstep #3: "If you're born gay, it can't be wrong to be gay."

[1]Julie Bindel, *Straight Expectations: What Does It Mean to Be Gay Today?* (Norwich, UK: Guardian Books, 2014), 75.

[2]Alan Jacobs, *Original Sin: A Cultural History* (New York: HarperCollins, 2009), xiv.

[3]Ibid.

[4]Ibid.

[5]Richard B. Hays, *The Moral Vision of the New Testament: A Contemporary Introduction to New Testament Ethics* (New York: HarperOne, 1996), 390.

Misstep #4: "If it makes you happy, it must be right!"

[1]Timothy Keller, *The Reason for God: Belief in an Age of Skepticism* (New York: Dutton, 2008), 114.

[2]Timothy Keller with Kathy Keller, *The Meaning of Marriage: Facing the Complexities of Commitment with the Wisdom of God* (New York: Riverhead Books, 2011), 19.

[3]C. S. Lewis, *The Problem of Pain* (Fount, 1998), 37.

Misstep #5: "Sex is where true intimacy is found."

[1]Kate Wharton, *Single-Minded: Being Single, Whole and Living Life to the Full* (Oxford: Monarch, 2013), 173.

[2]Andrew Sullivan, *Love Undetectable: Notes on Friendship, Sex, and Survival* (New York: Vintage, 1999), 199.

[3]Ibid., 234.

[4]William M. Struthers, *Wired for Intimacy: How Pornography Hijacks the Male Brain* (Downers Grove, IL: InterVarsity Press, 2009), 185.

[5]Paul David Tripp, *Broken-Down House: Living Productively in a World Gone Bad* (Wapwallopen, PA: Shepherd Press, 2009), 152.

[6]Anne Lamott, *Plan B: Further Thoughts on Faith* (New York: Riverhead Books, 2005), 174.

[7]Vaughan Roberts, *True Friendship: Walking Shoulder to Shoulder* (Leyland, UK: 10Publishing, 2013).

Misstep #6: "Men and women are equal and interchangeable."

[1]Dorothy L. Sayers, "The Human-Not-Quite-Human," in *Are Women Human? Astute and Witty Essays on the Role of Women in Society* (Grand Rapids: Eerdmans, 2005), 53.

[2]Ibid., 68.

[3]Christopher West, *Fill These Hearts: God, Sex, and the Universal Longing* (New York: Image, 2012), 11.

[4]Matthew Schmitz, "N. T. Wright on Gay Marriage," last modified June 11, 2014, www.firstthings.com/blogs/firstthoughts/2014/06/n-t-wrights -argument-against-same-sex-marriage.

[5]C. S. Lewis, "Priestesses in the Church?," in *Essay Collection: Faith, Christianity and the Church* (New York: HarperCollins, 2002), 401.

[6]Christopher C. Roberts, *Creation and Covenant: The Significance of Sexual Difference in the Moral Theology of Marriage* (New York: T & T Clark, 2007), 237.

[7]Melinda Selmys, *Sexual Authenticity: An Intimate Reflection on Homosexuality and Catholicism* (Huntington, IN: Our Sunday Visitor Publishing, 2009), 117.

[8]John Piper, "Sex and the Supremacy of Christ: Part One," in John Piper and Justin Taylor, eds., *Sex and the Supremacy of Christ* (Wheaton, IL: Crossway, 2005), 26.

Misstep #7: "Godliness is heterosexuality."

[1]Jenell Williams Paris, *The End of Sexual Identity: Why Sex Is Too Important to Define Who We Are* (Downers Grove, IL: InterVarsity Press, 2011), 87.

[2]Timothy Keller, *Counterfeit Gods: When the Empty Promises of Love, Money and Power Let You Down* (New York: Dutton, 2009), 64-66.

[3]See Andrew Goddard and Glynn Harrison, *Unwanted Same-Sex Attraction: Issues of Pastoral and Counselling Support* (London: Christian Medical Fellowship, 2011).

[4]Mark A. Yarhouse, *Homosexuality and the Christian: A Guide for Parents, Pastors, and Friends* (Bloomington, MN: Bethany House, 2010), 186.

[5]Dietrich Bonhoeffer, *Life Together* (London: SCM Press, 1954), 88.

Misstep #8: "Celibacy is bad for you."

[1]Christopher Ash, *Married for God: Making Your Marriage the Best It Can Be* (Nottingham, UK: Inter-Varsity Press, 2007), 41.

[2]One of the readers of this book suggested that Mary Poppins is the one example: she and Bert were "just good friends."

[3]See Al Hsu, *Singles at the Crossroads* (Downers Grove, IL: InterVarsity Press, 1997) for a great explanation of the fact that *everyone* who is not married has the gift of singleness that Paul is talking about here.

[4]Stanley Hauerwas, "Sex in Public: How Adventurous Christians Are Doing It," in Luke Bretherton and Russell Rook, eds., *Living Out Loud: Conversations About Virtue, Ethics and Evangelicalism* (Milton Keynes, UK: Paternoster, 2010), 182.

[5]Christopher West, *Fill These Hearts: God, Sex, and the Universal Longing* (New York: Image, 2012), 172.

Misstep #9: "Suffering is to be avoided."

[1]"I Asked the Lord that I Might Grow," written in 1779 by John Newton (1725–1807).

[2]Thomas Brooks, *Precious Remedies Against Satan's Devices* (Edinburgh: Banner of Truth, 1984), 115.

[3]John Flavel, *Keeping the Heart* (Ross-shire, UK: Christian Heritage, 1999), 40.

[4]William Still, "A Pastoral Perspective on Our Fallen Sexuality," in David Searle, ed., *Truth and Love in a Sexually Disordered World* (Ross-Shire, UK: Christian Focus, 2006), 63.

[5]C. S. Lewis, *The Great Divorce* (London: Fount, 1977), 8.

[6]C. S. Lewis, *The Silver Chair* (London: Puffin, 1965), 204.

[7]J. R. R. Tolkien, *The Lord of the Rings* (London: George Allen & Unwin, 1968), 988.

Conclusion

[1]Henri J. M. Nouwen, *The Wounded Healer: Ministry in Contemporary Society* (New York: Image, 1994), 86.

Appendix 1: The Plausibility of the Traditional Interpretation of Scripture

[1]Wesley Hill, *Washed and Waiting: Reflections on Christian Faithfulness and Homosexuality* (Grand Rapids: Zondervan, 2010), 61.

[2]Morna D. Hooker. "Adam in Romans 1," in *From Adam to Christ: Essays in Paul* (Eugene, OR: Wipf & Stock, 2008), 78.

[3]Simon J. Gathercole, "Sin in God's Economy: Agencies in Romans 1 and 7," in John M. G. Barclay and Simon J. Gathercole, eds., *Divine and Human Agency in Paul and His Cultural Environment* (New York: T & T Clark, 2008), 164.

[4]Sally Lloyd-Jones, *The Jesus Storybook Bible* (Grand Rapids: Zondervan, 2007), 16.

[5]C. S. Lewis, "The Weight of Glory," in *The C. S. Lewis Essay Collection: Faith, Christianity and the Church* (New York: HarperCollins, 2002), 104.

Appendix 2: The Implausibility of the New Interpretations of Scripture

[1]Matthew Vines, *God and the Gay Christian: The Biblical Case in Support of Same-Sex Relationships* (New York: Convergent Books, 2014), 158.

[2]Ibid., 17.

[3]Justin Lee, *Unconditional: Rescuing the Gospel from the Gay-vs-Christians Debate* (London: Hodder & Stoughton, 2012), 168.

[4]James V. Brownson, *Bible, Gender, Sexuality: Reframing the Church's Debate on Same-Sex Relationships* (Grand Rapids: Eerdmans, 2013), 9.

[5]Jeffrey John, *Permanent, Faithful, Stable: Christian Same-Sex Marriage* (London: Darton, Longman & Todd, 2012), 12.

[6]Morna D. Hooker. "Adam in Romans 1," in *From Adam to Christ: Essays in Paul* (Eugene, OR: Wipf & Stock, 2008), 78.

[7]Simon J. Gathercole, "Sin in God's Economy: Agencies in Romans 1 and 7," in John M. G. Barclay and Simon J. Gathercole, eds., *Divine and Human Agency in Paul and His Cultural Environment* (New York: T & T Clark, 2008), 165.

[8]Brownson, *Bible, Gender, Sexuality*, 156-161.

[9]John, *Permanent, Faithful, Stable*, 14.

[10]Ibid., 15.

[11]"Of the Authority of the Church," Article XX of the Thirty-Nine Articles of Religion as found in *The Book of Common Prayer*.

[12]Brownson, *Bible, Gender, Sexuality*, 79.

[13]Matthew Parris, "No, God would not have approved of gay bishops," *The Times*, August 9, 2003.

[14]See C. S. Lewis, *The Last Battle*.

Acknowledgments

[1]Sally Fitzgerald, ed., *The Habit of Being: The Letters of Flannery O'Connor* (New York: Vintage, 1980), 242.